Concealed Deception

*A Courageous Woman's Journey
from Abuse to Triumph*

Debra Williamson
with **Fred Williamson**

Vivid Publishing House
ATLANTA, GEORGIA

Concealed Deception:

A Courageous Woman's Journey from Abuse to Triumph

For more information, contact the publisher:

Vivid Publishing House
P.O. Box 360656
Decatur, GA 30036
vividpublishing.design@comcast.net

Library of Congress Card Catalogue Number: 20079312341
ISBN: 978-0-615-16894-4
First Printing: November 2007
Printed in Canada

DEDICATION
(Debra Williamson)

This book is dedicated to my mother, Gloria Williamson, who is the inspirational force behind my life. You taught and instilled in me the knowledge of God. This book is dedicated to you because of all the love, moral support, blessings, prayers and strength you gave me throughout life. All of these factors helped to bring me to this stage in my life, thus, making this book possible. I love you!

WHAT OTHERS ARE SAYING ABOUT
'Concealed Deception'

"This book is important and well worth reading. I've laid to rest many battered women. Maybe, just maybe, if they'd read *Concealed Deception*, perhaps they would've been here to share their story."

- *Willie Watkins, Watkins Funeral Service*
  (Mortician for Coretta Scott King)

"Out of my 30 years of experience, I've had to perform plastic surgery on hundreds of women who've been battered from domestic violence. After reading *Concealed Deception*, I'm so happy that my dear friend Debra didn't make it to my operating table. I must say that I am so proud of this courageous and brave woman for rising up above the affliction of abuse and sharing her testimony to many in need of counseling. Debra's story provides a lesson for every woman who may or may not have gone through what she did."

- *Dr. Leroy Loving, D.D.S. and M.D.*

"This absorbing book showed Debra Williamson at close range – a luminous woman of great warmth and high purpose who has led a fascinating and often inspiring life."

- *John Christmas, Entertainment Attorney*

"The challenges that women face at the hands of abusive men are horrific, to say the least. In *Concealed Deception*, Debra Williamson freely shares the personal struggles she experienced during her quest to live happily ever after. The good news is that, in the midst of all that she endured, she came out victorious. Debra shares her story in a compelling manner that will be of great encouragement to any woman who has ever suffered the evils of abuse."

- *Vincent Fort, Georgia State Senator*

"Boldness and courage are the two words that exemplify the sentiment of what is shared in Debra Williamson's captivating work, *Concealed Deception*. I know firsthand of what victims experience because I too have been in the hands of an abuser. This book has sparked joy and pain, but most importantly, it has helped me to have more faith in God. Now I'm delivered from the bondage I've had for many years. Read *Concealed Deception* and be set free."

- Debbie Berry, Edible Art Catering

"As an avid reader, many stories have touched my heart but none quite like *Concealed Deception*. Domestic violence has become an epidemic in this country. Hundreds of child abuse cases have come across my desk, and in many cases, physical abuse has led to the death of someone in the household. Women and their children are affected each and every day for the rest of their lives. Please save a life, and read *Concealed Deception*."

- Ernestine Cole, Director
Department of Family and Children Services

"Wow, what an awesome book. I've never experienced domestic violence, but out of all my years in the school system, I have looked into the eyes of many unhappy children and their parents who are faced with domestic violence. After reading *Concealed Deception*, I make it a point to handle all the students with care so they can at least have a good learning experience and go on to become someone great like Debra."

- Valerie Swinton, Principal
Cedar Grove Elementary School

"I am amazed that my dear friend Debra Williamson has endured so much pain and sorrow and somehow still is able to rise above the wreckage, share her heartfelt story, and save others. Debra is truly a courageous woman. I commend you, Debra, for all of your works."

- Cindra K.Taylor, Vice President
National Black Child Development Association

DEBRA WILLIAMSON'S ACKNOWLEDGMENTS

All honor, power and glory be to the Lord God Almighty and His beloved son, Jesus, who gave me the strength to make it through all the dark and difficult days I endured in my life. Thank you for making this book possible.

To my wonderful, wise and loving mother, whom I would not trade for all the riches of the world. You've helped make me into the woman I am today, and you taught me how to be a loving mother. I love you from the depths of my heart.

To my daughter, Diamond Parker, my bundle of joy, who brings happiness to the hearts of everyone around her. I love you, precious!

I want to give great thanks and gratitude to my siblings — Carlton Williamson, Kenny Bain Williamson, Oliver Dilligard, Valerie Braxton and Fred Williamson — for their love, strength and encouragement, which inspired me to write this book.

To all my relatives and friends in the United States and in the Bahamas, special thanks for all the love and support I received from you.

To my dear friends, Connie Irish, Martha King, Charlotte Ferrell, Liz Morand and my wonderful loving cousins Patti Ferguson, Monique Ferguson, Corlette and Earl Deveaux, thanks for your great support throughout my ups and downs and for always being there when I needed you.

I would also like to thank Alonia Jernigan and Annette Johnson for their expertise in editing. I appreciate their insight in helping to assure that everything in the book was presented with clarity and integrity. You both are greatly appreciated.

An extra special thanks to my brother, Fred Williamson, because you were more than willing to take on the difficult task of helping me write and put this book together. I appreciate and cherish you. Thanks again for your hard work and many long nights of staying up to write.

FRED WILLIAMSON'S
ACKNOWLEDGMENTS

First and foremost, I would like to thank God Almighty and Jesus Christ, my Lord, for allowing me the wonderful opportunity to help write Debra's book. It took prayer to get past certain parts of this book because it broke my heart and caused anger and sadness when I learned of the abuse Debra faced and endured.

I would like to thank Gloria Williamson, my beautiful mother, who encouraged me with such kind words every time we talked about the making of this book.

To my son and daughter, Gary S. Williamson and Jazmin A. Williamson, I love you very much! Thanks for your love, understanding and prayers.

Thanks to Mr. Daniel Greene, who encourages me to better myself daily. Thanks for your class, "Don't Sweat the Small Stuff!"

To my friends, Christian brothers and sisters who inspired me to keep writing in the face of obstacles, thank you: John Jerry, Michelle Pinkston, Fernando Garcia, Fernando Ware, Terri Williams, John Davis (B.K.), Michael Williams, Robert Young (Robbo), Julius Cabell, Houston Grant, Tommy Waddell, Clarence Lucas, Darryl Bryant, Josh Edmond, Darrell and Peggie Wells, Tom Ellis, David Altman, Curtina F. Rahming, Tracy Grant, Shannon Charlton, Ava Brown, Leo Harrington, and my main man from Chicago, "Jalal."

To my brother Bobby Atmore and his wife, Yvette, words cannot describe the depth of love I have for you. I love you as my own soul.

To my two brothers in Christ Jesus, who have been my inspiration, my mentors, father figures and my great support, Thirkel Freeman and Ramon G. Morell. I love you more than words can ever express. Thank you for sharing your love and family with me.

To Michael Tyre (a.k.a. Chucky), my writing partner, dear close friend, my brother whom I love deeply. Thanks, Mike, for inspiring me to keep writing as we bring our joint projects to life. You're going to make Laurel, Delaware proud!

Finally, thanks to my wonderful sister, Debra Williamson, for giving me the privilege of being a part of helping to writing this book. It was my pleasure!

CONTENTS

INTRODUCTION

Writing this book opened old wounds that I hoped to heal at its completion. It took a lot of pain to write, and its contents are written in heart-heaviness and tears. There were periods of time when I had to put down the pen and stop writing because tears flowed uncontrollably from my eyes.

Parts of my life were darkly faded and blurry. Sometimes it seemed as though a whirlwind tunnel of confusion surrounded me. It caused me to forget exact times and events, so I decided to write this book in the form of a fictional adaptation based on actual events in my life and sketches of my imagination. Even though some of the events are fictitious, they are not far from the actual truth of my life.

PROLOGUE

As a little girl, I remember being outside and looking up in the clear night sky before going into the house. The stars sparkled as I wondered about the vastness overhead. I thought of my little life and where I fit in this big world. I thought about how my life compared to other people's life around me, and I wondered about the life of all the people I couldn't see. Throughout life, I often closed my eyes and pictured that scene of me standing under the star-studded skies and wondering, "Which way do I go now?"

It was the summer of the year I turned eight years old, and life finally began to make a little sense. Being a little black girl growing up in a low income neighborhood in Fort Lauderdale, Florida without a father was somewhat confusing before I came of age and was able to put one and two together. My father, Amos Williamson, born and raised in the Caribbean Islands, stood about 5'10," bore a dark complexion, and was much older than my mother. Being married, living in the United States and becoming an American citizen, my father then divorced his wife and decided he wanted a younger wife. Amos went back home to Nassau, Bahamas where my mother, Gloria Deveaux lived at the time, though she was born in Acklins Island Bahamas. Amos married my mother making her Mrs. Gloria Williamson and brought her to Hallandale, Florida to live.

My father lived about ten miles away in Hallandale, Florida. When Mom and Dad broke up, he made little effort to spend quality time with the kids. At the time, Mom had four children from my father, which she took care of all by herself. Life held a lot of mysteries for me, but I knew life had a lot to offer; I wanted my share of the good things.

15

Gloria Williamson, at the time, was in her mid 30s. Very short, my mom and I stand about the same height, around 4'11". Mom is a shade darker than milk chocolate while my complexion is a shade lighter than milk chocolate. Mom has high cheek bones and deep African features. She is an extraordinary woman who ended up raising six children on her own. She sacrificed to make sure everyone in the family was provided for. Though we didn't have the best of everything in life, we had everything needed to live day by day. Often, I wondered how Mom made it alone. One day she said to me, "Baby, the Lord is my husband, and He always makes a way somehow." Throughout my life, those words have remained in my heart.

Kenny, my youngest brother, hadn't been born yet, and my father was nowhere in sight. Gloria Williamson was the only mother and father I knew. The only memory I have of my father is when he was sick in the hospital, then he died. The only time I saw his face after he got sick was at his funeral. During the early 70s, the hospital where my father was admitted only allowed adults to visit the sick, so children had to stay outside to play at a supervised playground.

Though I missed having a father and having a strong male presence in my life, his death didn't really cause me any pain or grief at that stage of my life. In my mind, his existence is like a faded dream that I can't put in scenes or explain clearly.

Missing a father I never had around, or didn't even know, felt strange, but I kept all my thoughts and feelings closed up inside. Somehow during my young age, I knew having a strong positive male figure was important to have in life. A part of me craved for a father's presence while the other part of me seemed not to care. Because of my young age, I wasn't able to put all things together concerning a man's true role in a family. In a sense, I think my

16

two oldest brothers, Carlton and Fred, fulfilled part of the missing male/father presence in my life. My brother, Oliver (Junior), was only a baby at the time. So since I was the youngest child, life remained a little tricky and confusing because Fred always tried to pick fights with me, play nasty tricks, or lead me into some kind of trouble with him. Carlton, the oldest child (now 5'10" and the same complexion as my mother), constantly found himself defending me or protecting me from Fred. Carlton was so cool and laid back, yet he possessed the sternness to rescue me so often from Fred just in the nick of time. I really admired Carlton, and so did many others. His friends thought he was so cool they nicknamed him Chilly.

Looking back, now I understand that living in a house full of kids inevitably would produce squabbling and sibling rivalries, but I had no idea that these encounters would later be re-enacted as a pattern of the horrible, abusive life I would face in the future. When I became an adult and got married, I thought I had begun a road to achieving the good things life had to offer. But as life went on, I tasted the sour and bitter back side of life's hand by being abused by a man who claimed to love me.

My young life proved interesting because something was always going on between my siblings and me. My oldest sister, Valerie, (about 5'1" with beautiful skin the color of mocha and bow-legged), added balance to my sense of thinking from a woman's perspective. She seemed very strong and tough, even mean at times. Yet, she was kind, gentle, feminine and loving. What I really liked about Valerie was her willingness to stand in crisis, and the fact that she never backed down from anyone. She was a fighter, and I was determined to be a fighter also.

Fred, now 5'11" and my complexion, could be kind and affectionate in his own special way, but mainly he was just a young boy being a boy. When he wasn't trying to beat up on me, he picked fights with Valerie. When Fred made her mad, she would yell, "Stop, you red dog!"

Fred yelled back, "Who you calling a red dog, you black tar baby!" Then the fighting would begin and a series of punches would be thrown. Not long after, Fred and Carlton would be going at it. Being the little sister, I had to devise my own technique to survive. I became the master of "Hit and Run." I'd get one good punch in during a fight, and then take off running for the room, locking the door so no one could get in.

That whole phase of growing up with brothers and a sister added its share of confusion also. I couldn't quite understand or comprehend how, at times, my siblings and I could show each other so much love and affection, and a day later we'd be back to fighting like cats and dogs. My confusion remained fueled by fighting with those you love or those who are supposed to love you. Later on in life during my relationship with men, that same type of confusion thrived and stayed unresolved in my heart and in my way of thinking. Somewhere in the back of my mind during my abusive marriage, I felt our relationship would, in time, evolve into a healthy one, the same as my relationships with my siblings did.

Through all the confusion as a child, Mom maintained balance in our home when she was around. She kept love flowing through the family even in the midst of the hard times life offered. She constantly stressed to the children the importance of loving and respecting each other even though the fighting continued. I know, at times, the children had Mom wanting to pull her hair out. Her hard labor of love and motherhood paid off in the long run because as the children grew older, the fighting stopped. We all became close and shared so much love and respect for each other. We all remain close until this very day.

Many years would pass before I really understood the importance and impact of the void in my life I felt by not growing up with a father. I did feel the older I became the less I missed or thought of my father, but the feeling of life cheating me out of a parent accompanied me and refused to leave.

There were parts in my young life where Mom got involved in relationships with men, hoping to find a good husband and stepfather for her children. At first, the men appeared nice—-I mean the perfect gentlemen. But, in the middle or towards the end of the relationship, the kind loving gentleman's role would have all changed for the worse. This type of behavior also left me troubled and baffled in mind. It was hard to see a man treat my Mom with so much love and respect, then a year later watch the same man try to beat up on her or say very nasty and horrible things to her. All these things further affected me. For a while, I almost thought such treatment was how a relationship should be between a man and a woman.

To make matters worse and even more confusing, I began to be physically abused by one of Mom's mates named Pete. At first, I felt protected by him, but later I was at a point of fearing him. One day, Pete beat me with a belt as though he hated me, leaving a few visible marks on my body. He abused Mom several times to the point where she feared to say anything about the way he beat me. I knew there were several times when she bit her tongue, hating to see how he beat me. I think she hated it even more that she was unable to do anything about it. Eventually, Mom worked up the nerves to stand up against Pete and end the relationship.

I remember one day when I was six years old, and Mom came home from work. Cartoons were on television, and I sat glued to the tube. She walked in the front door, and began giving out commands to do house chores. I could hear and sense a bit of excitement in Mom's voice, "Okay kids, Mommie is having company over today——I want everyone to help clean the house. I want y'all to be on your best behavior when you meet him. Fred, I need you to take out the trash. You and Carlton clean up the yard and cut the grass. Valerie and Debra, I want you to clean up the kitchen and living room. I'll clean the bathrooms."

My little mind——always so inquisitive——clicked and searched for answers, "Mommie, are we going to get a new daddy?"

She smiled, "I don't know yet...maybe."

Fred asked, "Mommie, what time is he supposed to come?"

Smiling, Mom answered, "Around seven o'clock."

Mom's smile faded when, surprisingly, Fred said in defiance, "I don't want no new daddy; my daddy is dead..."

Mom's smile further declined as Valerie added her two cents, "I don't want no other man telling me what to do..."

Mom interrupted to calm everyone down before we all spilled our unwelcome opinions and revealed our rejecting hearts before her, "Everybody calm down and take it easy...please just be nice when he comes over."

Carlton asked, "Mommie, what's his name?"

Mom answered, "His name is Julian."

We all met Julian, and after he gave all the kids a dollar bill, we liked him. Eventually, he moved in with us. Over the next year, Julian seemed nice, but he slowly changed to a mean-spirited man. One night, Julian came home drunk, and I heard him and Mom in the bedroom arguing and then fighting. I sat in my room wondering what was happening, and hoping Mom got the upper hand in the fight. To my disappointment, the next day Mom told us, "Julian almost choked me to death."

After Julian and Mom had a fight, Julian would leave and disappear for several days then come back home begging and apologizing. But this time around, Mom decided that things would have to be different. She knew she would need help to overpower this man, or things would just continue to get worse between them during their battles. So one day at the dinner table when Julian wasn't there, she said, "Kids, every time you all see or hear me fighting, none of you come to my rescue to help me. But the next time y'all don't help me fight, I'm gonna just stop feeding you."

A week later, he and Mom were back together going about life as though nothing happened. One night during that same week, Julian came home drunk, and decided to jump on Mom while she was in the kitchen preparing dinner. They started arguing, and the argument drifted into the living room where all the kids were watching television. As soon as Julian grabbed Mom, all the kids attacked him, remembering what Mom said early on about not feeding us. We grabbed and threw objects at him. Fred went into the kitchen and came back with a butter knife. Because all the kids were so small, Julian slung us one by one over the living room. Fred threw the butter knife at Julian, but missed. By the time Julian went to grab Mom again, he was a little exhausted. Mom sat on the couch leaning back with her feet propped up like a snake's head ready to strike. When Julian reached close enough, Mom took both feet and thrust them into his chest, sending him smashing into the wall like he had been hit with a bolt of lightening. Julian got up from the floor, got in his car and left the house.

I can't remember exactly how Mom and Julian broke up. All I remember is one day he stepped into our lives, and one day he was gone like a vapor, which was fine with me; I never asked

Mom what happened to him. For the next couple of years, I watched Mom live her life before me struggling to make it on her own. By watching Mom's actions, a seed took root in me to live and survive with or without a man in my life.

At eleven years old, I noticed a deep spiritual stirring within me. At the time, I really didn't know exactly what it was. I'm blessed to have a mother who took time out to teach all her children the Lord's Prayer, Psalms 23 and how to pray. Each one of us had to memorize everything she taught us. Something inside often reminded me that my destiny is to be successful and prosperous, both physically and spiritually. A strong drive developed inside to fulfill that part of my life. Somehow I knew the intuition was connected with the spiritual stirring taking place inside my heart. Later in life, I learned how real and obtainable my quests were, and that it would take hard work, sacrifices, pain and dedication to achieve.

Mom provided a spiritual base and religious platform in our home. She constantly instilled in her children the love of God, and about the teachings and knowledge of Jesus Christ. It wouldn't be until later in life that I really learned to lean and depend on the Lord. A series of events had taken place in my life, and had not Mom taught me about faith in Jesus Christ and the tender mercies of God, I wouldn't have had anything to fall back on during my times of trials and crisis.

Mom made customized draperies for a living. She taught all the children how to sew, and she made sure we took pride in our work. Taking pride in what I did became a principle which took me a long way in life. Mom sat all the children down one day and told us, "If you're going to take out time to do something, always do your best. Take pride in your work because if you are not planning on doing your best, there's no need in doing it." I mended her advice into my way of life, and I truly believe that had it not been for her giving my siblings and me a firm foundation upon which to build, my ability to endure and overcome the spousal abuse — verbal, mental and physical — would not have been possible. My prayer is that *Concealed Deception* will be a source of inspiration, courage and hope for those who have had to face spousal abuse, as well as the people who love them.

Victoriously,
Debra Williamson

Chapter 1

HIGH SCHOOL AND COLLEGE

I'm trapped in a moving capsule, and I'm being carried upside down. I don't know how I'm surviving, but it seems that everything needed for life is with me. I've been kicking and pushing against the elastic type surface for awhile, but everywhere I push with my hands and feet, the rubbery material rebounds to its original shape. There's a strong force outside this warm dark bubble I'm in, but I don't know what it is. I curl up, naked as a jay bird, feeling the ground trembling underneath my head.

The outer force stops moving so I lay quiet listening to a soft thumping rhythm, wondering what is going on overhead as the rhythm inside the capsule changes, and the outer sound of a slight commotion begins overhead. Something is going on, but I don't know what it is.

My surrounding bubble presses me then releases its pressure. This condition persists as I keep sliding back and forth. The pressure at my feet grows stronger and stronger, gradually pushing me forward until my head presses hard against the capsule's wall. Even though there's a lot of turbulence, there is no fear inside me because the gel covers and protects me, absorbing any shock that enters my space.

As the force keeps gaining momentum, I realize something has to give. Either the capsule bursts open or my neck breaks. I can feel the capsule gathering strength ready to render another powerful thrust. Wow! There it goes again! My head penetrates the capsule's wall that provided a small hole for my head to slowly slip through. The squeezing force behind me keeps pushing and pushing until it popped me out of the capsule. Astonished, I say to myself, "I have arrived! I don't know where I am... all I know is everything inside me says, 'I'm supposed to be here.'"

Air rushes through my nose, and it takes several seconds for my brain to register and adjust to the new technique of breathing. My vision is blurred as I dangle upside down while this six feet tall creature holds both my ankles with one hand. His free hand swings back then returns forward, smacking me on my naked buttocks. The stinging pain is trapped inside my body while my cry is trapped inside my throat. The man fans back his hand and spanks my buttocks again, and I let out a loud hard cry. Then is when I realize I am an infant born into the world.

My eyes pop open, releasing me back into reality; but my mind is still held captive as part of my dream while questions in my mind seem to filter down from nowhere, "Is this what I have to look forward to as I enter into this new world? What have I done to make the doctor keep hitting me like that? What kind of welcome and treatment is this?"

The questions continue as my mind slowly recovers back to its full state. I lie curled up in a fetal position as the dream replays in my mind, and I wonder if my birth actually happened the way I dreamt it.

I can't help but wonder what was happening to me, what or who is behind my dreams and what it is trying to tell or show me. My dreams left me with questions and a lot of soul searching. I continue living in this unknown world of my own, filled with unanswered questions and weird dreams.

Starting high school in 1978 created a whole new set of challenges. My best friend, Tasha Brown, and I attended Dillard High School together. We had already attended elementary and middle school together. We watched each other grow into womanhood, and we were the first to recognize each other's interest in boys. We even experienced having our first menstrual cycle about the same time.

I remember the day of my first menstrual cycle. Strolling down the hallway at Lauderdale Lakes Middle School, Tasha walked up behind me striding step for step. She walked a centimeter behind me with only enough space for air to come between us. I know some of the students were thinking, "What in the world…" Breathing down the back of my neck Tasha said, "Debra girl, keep walking straight to the ladies room. You have a big red spot showing in the middle of your butt. Girl, your period is on and you picked a fine day to wear white pants." Luckily, we had a teacher at school who knew exactly what to do. Tasha comforted me by letting me know there was nothing to worry about and that she also had her period two days ago. Mom had already talked to Valerie and me about feminine things, but I guess I wasn't expecting my period so soon. From that day on, Tasha and I kept tampons in our purse. We both carried an extra tampon just in case the other person needed one.

Like most close girlfriends, our relationship was tested by the ultimate tester, a boy! Unfortunately, we happened to like the same boy in high school. His name was Terrence Moss, and he was the cutest and most handsome little man at Dillard. He was tall and dark with a hypnotizing appeal, and he also happened to be the school's basketball star. Every time Terrence passed by, Tasha and I gave him our best girly pose and prettiest facial expression, hoping to grab and arrest his attention.

As Terrence passed, I said, "Ooouu Tasha, did you see how he smiled at me?"

Tasha replied, "Child please, Debra. He was smiling at me. Our eyes were locked together like link chains."

I sucked my teeth, "Yeah right…"

I turned my back to Tasha. It was obvious to Terrence we both liked him. He would always pass by us and smile while walking in an arrogant innocence, knowing he was "all of that!" I guess, like most boys, he couldn't resist the temptation to test out the newly discovered power he had over surrendering girls.

One day at lunch, I noticed Terrence walking toward my table with his lunch tray. I sat alone figuring Terrence would walk by and smile as usual. I was shocked and surprised as he stopped and asked, "Can I sit here and have lunch with you?"

Almost at a loss for words, they stumbled out of my mouth, "Sure…uh…yes. Go ahead…uh yeah you can seat—I mean have a seat."

Terrence recognized my nervousness and with two big ocean sized grins we smiled at each other.

"So what's your name," he asked.

"Debra. My name is Debra Williamson," I answered, nearly forgetting my name because of my unrestrained blushing.

"My name is—." Before Terrence could get his name out, I blurted, "Terrence, right?"

He smiled and asked, "How do you know my name?"

Embarrassingly, I answered, "Don't play crazy. You know that every girl in this school knows who you are."

He replied as though he was told something he didn't know, "Oh yeah, you think so?"

Terrence stared at me with the most attractive and charming smile, "Debra, you're a beautiful young lady. I noticed you the very first day of school." Even though I sat thinking Terrence probably used the same pickup line on every girl he first met, it didn't matter because he took my breath away with his up close presence. I let him continue with the much welcomed compliments, "I like the way you fix your hair and the way you dress. You got style." I basked in the moment of having the one who was the topic of conversation for every girl in school, the most popular guy at Dillard, hitting on me.

All I could think to say was, "Uh...thanks. Thanks for the compliments..."

At a total loss for words, I sat silent and satisfied when Terrence broke the quietness, "What are the chances of getting your phone number?"

Trying not to show any excitement I responded, "Well, you can get it if you promise to call me."

"That's no problem," he said, "You got my word. I promise to call you."

I asked, "Do you have something to write with?" There was no way I could finish eating my lunch with Terrence sitting in front of me; I had so much going on inside my stomach. My insides were spilling over with butterflies. I gave him my telephone number and came up with a little white lie to get away from the table. I didn't want to start falling apart and chance losing Terrence's interest. Coming up with a quick lie I said, "Um...Excuse me, Terrence. I'm supposed to meet my friend, Tasha." I didn't feel too bad about the little lie because I did have to meet Tasha; she just didn't know we had to meet. I had to meet Tasha to boast of my encounter with Terrence.

Calmly, I walked away from the lunch table with every intention to go hunt down Tasha. She stood at the school's concession counter buying a hot dog, Coke and Snicker's bar. My eyes, bubbling with joy, prompted Tasha to ask, "Girl, what are you so perky about?"

I couldn't wait to tell Tasha, "Girl, guess who asked for my telephone number?"

Tasha shook her head and said, "Uh, uh...not Terrence!"

More than eager to answer I replied, "Yep, you're right...Terrence."

Tasha said jokingly, "I can't believe it. I had plans of marrying that fool."

Tasha slapped me five and said, "You go, girl! I got to step off 'cause you got the prize." We hugged in a sneak celebration, and then we walked to class.

Terrence called me and we spent the next week talking on the telephone and learning things about each other. The following week, we shared our first kiss and on the same day, Tasha brought me unwanted news, "Debra, girl, we got to talk."

In Tasha's face, I could see something wasn't right. "What's up, Tasha," I asked.

She answered, "It's your boy Terrence."

My heart dropped, "Terrence, what's wrong with Terrence?"

Tasha poked out her lips and said, "Nothing is wrong with Terrence. That fool saw me in the hallway, gave me his phone number and asked me to call him."

I stood not knowing what to say, but I managed to squeak out a few words through the pressing lump in my throat, "So what you gonna do?"

Tasha paused and looked at me in pity as though she waited for the answer to come from me, "Debra, you my girl. The offer was tempting, but I can't do you like that." At that moment, I felt Tasha became my true friend for life. She passed the ultimate test. Tasha continued, "Debra, I can't tell you what to do, but just remember Terrence ain't nothing but a dog—just like the rest of them. He doesn't deserve a woman like you." I couldn't say anything, but I agreed by nodding my head. I felt blessed and relieved Tasha didn't betray our friendship. Tasha and I ended up playing tricks on Terrence by giving him the "Royal Run-a-round." Tasha pretended as though she didn't tell me about Terrence's proposal for her to call him. Terrence finally caught on and got the message after setting dates at separate times to meet me or Tasha somewhere and we never showed up. We lost Terrence's charming smiles and sexy stares, but more importantly, Tasha and I kept our close friendship.

After graduating from high school and preparing for college, leaving home created one of the saddest days of my life. Going off to Hampton University and not having Tasha come with me was very hard. Tasha stayed home in Fort Lauderdale after high school and attended Broward Community College. I received a two year academic scholarship and took advantage of a grant that allowed me to attend college for four years, majoring in business administration. The day I stepped on the airplane headed for Hampton University in the state of Virginia, I felt like I was leaving a part of me behind. Tasha would be missed dearly.

Walking on Hampton University's campus felt like being a piece of meat displayed on an auction block. Everyone was staring at me because they saw I was a new face. Guys whistled and made boyish remarks.

As I looked around, I thought, "This school is not what I pictured it to be." Added to my already dislike of the campus, the college sat in the middle of a low income neighborhood. Dillard High School was situated the same way, and I felt like I was starting high school all over again. To make matters even worse, I started missing Tasha more than ever. Despite my initial dissatisfaction of the new surroundings, I made up my mind and promised myself to focus on getting a degree and strive towards set goals.

Determined to make the best of the next four years at Hampton, I concentrated on my studies. Making friends always came easy for me, but for some reason, I experienced separation from the norm around the campus. Students gathered in small groups talking, laughing and running around. The atmosphere seemed a bit childish and the excitement for some students breaking free from home was written all over their faces. It was obvious they enjoyed being away from their parents' supervision. My thinking and purpose had gone beyond what I saw, and there was little room in me for a childish mindset—I was on a mission. Most of my time was spent in classes or in my room reading or studying.

I couldn't believe my eyes once I arrived at Hampton and was escorted to a dorm room. The rooms were the size of a wardrobe closet. I stood at the door wanting to turn around and go home. Sitting inside the room was a young lady named Carla Ware, who made arriving at Hampton much easier for me. They couldn't have given me a better roommate. Carla was very kind and she gave me the warmest welcome one could give considering the circumstances. Carla was a pretty girl. She was tall and lanky with a soft caramel skin complexion, sandy light brown hair hanging at her neck line, and a beautiful face sporting unique bone structure. She looked like a black version of Michelle Pfeiffer, and she had the intelligence to go with her looks.

Being friends with Carla made attending Hampton worthwhile. In a way, she filled the void in my heart that came from missing Tasha. Tasha was still my girl and my best friend of all, but Carla and I became very close. We shared some of the same interests and ideas. In many ways, we were alike. We had the same major in college, the same view about family values, moral standards, politics and religion. Carla's main focus was similar to mine: getting a good education so we could return home to execute plans and accomplish goals previously set.

As time passed, Carla and I became closer friends and stuck

together like glue. Only one argument ensued between us the whole time we were together. The arguments were caused because Carla tried to force me into eating some food when I got sick. Two days had passed without me eating anything. Carla begged, "Please, Debra, eat something. Even though you don't have an appetite, you have to eat something."

I refused several times, but she persisted until I screamed, "Leave me alone. I'm not hungry!" Carla turned and walked away like I had really hurt her feelings, only to return with a bowl of delicious hot chicken soup mixed with vegetables. Then she sat down and spoon fed me.

We sat in our small room for hours sometimes exploring business ideas, sketching out proposals and talking about our future life. Carla's main interest was becoming a financial consultant and opening a real estate business. Real estate was one of my interests also, but my primary goal was to first open a hair salon and sell houses on the side. Styling hair was a love and passion for me. I enjoyed fixing Mom's and Valerie's hair before I went off to college. Tasha and I used to experiment with different hairstyles on each other's heads. My plans were to enroll in real estate school and cosmetology school immediately after graduating from Hampton University.

Thoughts of being successful haunted me. I welcomed the thoughts of hope because they kept me going during the times I felt like giving up. I always had the feeling God was with me. That, along with a burning drive inside, kept me working towards making accomplishments in life.

Somewhere in my college life, I knew the issue concerning

dating and boys had to be addressed and added into the equation of completing this part of my life. For a while, Carla and I did good by keeping each other focused on school work and not really thinking about relationships with boys. To make things more difficult, Carla and I befriended a young lady attending Hampton named Nikki Coleman. Nikki kept a stylish short haircut, which complimented her oval shaped face. She had a dark chocolate skin complexion and a body like a Coke bottle. Guys always greeted her with flirtatious comments and gestures as she approached them, "There she go… Nikki—small in the waist and cute in the face — damn, you're fine!" Nikki would smile and suck up every word with her body language as she strut by them. She was a likeable person with a gang of friends. All she constantly talked about was boys, boys, boys — always trying to hook up Carla and I with some guy. Nikki knew everybody's business: who dated who, and who was free game.

Although I liked Nikki, she became a big distraction for me. She always showed up in the middle of homework telling me who wanted to meet or talk to me. I would tell her how important it was for me to finish my homework or give her hints I wasn't interested, but she ignored them and kept going on and on talking like the Energizer Bunny. Carla and I were satisfied with fantasizing about what our future dream mate would be like. We both wanted the handsome, intellectual type man. Carla insisted on the tall basketball type, while I envisioned a mold or clone of Denzel Washington. Not only was I thinking about myself and career, but also about my future kids and what they would look like. I felt with my looks, accompanied with a Denzel look alike,

35

we would produce a flock of beautiful babies. I know it's somewhat vain to think that way, but that's how we ladies think sometimes.

One day while Carla reminded me how vain and shallow my thinking was about future kids, Nikki burst through our room door excited like she was a novice medical student who stumbled into a newly discovered cure for cancer, "Girls, girls, girls! Tomorrow night is fun time — the Q-Dogs are having a fraternity party and we have to be there!"

"I'm sorry," I replied as Carla followed my lead. "Me too."

Nikki begged, "Come on, guys, you should have fun sometime. For once, let's all go out together—pleeaase!" Carla looked at me and I looked at her as we both were thinking, "We are getting a little tired and bored with each other."

"Okay, I'll go," I said hesitantly.

Nikki started jumping for joy, but restrained herself until she got the same response from Carla, "Alright, we can hang—count me in." Nikki screamed and jumped up and down as though she had just won a brand new car on *The Price is Right* television game show.

We all decided to go and have as much fun as possible. I think we had more fun getting ready for the party than actually going. We helped each other get beautified. Months had passed since I last put on makeup and dressed up to go anywhere. I think a woman needs to dress up every now and then, even if she dresses up and stays at home feeling beautiful. Feeling the power of beauty inside and outside yourself builds confidence and self-esteem. I think every woman is beautiful in one way or the other.

Carla had a problem with her looks and I often assured her

that she was a beautiful person inside and out. She once explained to me one of the factors that helped shape her personality. She said, "I try to be nice to everyone and that helps compensate for what I lack in looks." I didn't tell her how ridiculous she sounded, but tried to understand her part of a woman's thinking. I thought, "Women can really come up with some strange things, or maybe she was constantly told at a young age she wasn't pretty. I guess that's what makes us different and unique from each other." Nonetheless, Carla's behavior stayed consistently humble and pleasant.

While at the party, we penetrated the dim, crowded room and pressed forward to find an empty space to stand and check out the scenes. Everyone at the fraternity party seemed to be having fun. Guys were flirting all over the place. Because there were so many guys from various parts of the country, I was introduced to a whole new world of "pickup lines." Many times, I laughed inside because of how ridiculous they sounded. Some girls fell for them. I was amazed at how crafty the guys were with words and the tools of flattery. Sometimes, I thought they must have practiced their pickup lines over and over until they knew it would ensure high percentage results. I had never been bombarded with such a litany of guys and pickup lines. This was a new experience for me. The only thing on the guys' mind that night was sex. Everyone who approached me was aggressive and acted like they wanted to eat me alive. The aggressive behavior wasn't my cup of tea.

Carla and I stood watching, not knowing what to do to have fun. This was our first fraternity party, but it appeared to be home for Nikki. The moment she entered the room, she fell right in place, bouncing around like a human pin-ball.

After an hour of standing, Carla and I looked for a place to sit. We joined a flowing circle of people walking around the poorly lit room looking for seats, but there were none empty. People literally sat on top of each other in chairs. We walked until we got tired then stopped and stood next to a guy named Shawn Percy. He smiled and spoke to us, "How are you ladies doing?"

Shawn looked directly in my face waiting for us to return the greeting. I said to myself, "Now, here's a guy that might interest me.

I responded with a smile, "I'm fine." Carla looked and gave me "the eyes." Shawn stood alone quietly, well-dressed and looking out of place like us. He tried to talk to me, but I could barely hear him because of the loud music. He offered to go outside and talk so we could get away from all the loud noise. I obliged him and we walked outside together leaving Carla standing alone. Right away, Shawn and I hit it off with mutual attraction. He had a dark brown complexion and was good looking with a contagious smile revealing straight white teeth to go along with his clean cut, black wavy hair and gentle appearance.

Shawn and I got together and we fell in love, but things got a bit complicated with sex coming into the picture and Shawn demanding a lot of my time. Every time Shawn and I had sex, the moral conviction came down heavy on me and I felt so bad afterward. This was not how I envisioned this part of my life. I agreed to go with the flow for the time being. Shawn didn't understand the fact that we couldn't spend every waking hour together. I wanted to end the relationship, but we ended up suffering along with each other until the four years at Hampton University approached its end. Deep down inside, we both knew we weren't ready to make any lasting commitments and plans to be together after college. Shawn lived in Michigan and I lived in Florida. In an unspoken way, we settled for our togetherness as something we had during college.

Somehow, the time zoomed by and four years didn't seem as long as anticipated.

Receiving a four-year business degree helped the pages of my life finally start to turn because at one point, during college my life, seemed to be standing still. College life wasn't an easy life for me.

I graduated from college and right away, I enrolled in cosmetology school. I decided to go to cosmetology school at night and during the day fix hair under apprenticeship to save money to pay for real estate school. I moved in with Mom and helped foot some of the bills. When I came home from college, I discovered Florida had good state grants for vocational schools. I took advantage of the benefits and enrolled at Wolford Hair Academy in Fort Lauderdale. Immediately after receiving my beautician license, I borrowed money from family and friends to open my own hair salon called Clinique Hair Studio. I rented building space in a strip plaza located on Hallandale Beach Boulevard in Hallandale.

Hallandale was only minutes south of Fort Lauderdale, creating no problems in commuting back and forth. I hired three licensed beauticians to work in the salon on commission.

Business didn't do as well as was expected. For one, the location was not conducive for a black hair styling business. Secondly, I didn't give the business a chance to blossom. After being open a year, Mom informed me of her plans to move to Georgia. I planned on staying in Fort Lauderdale and giving my hair salon a chance to grow until Mom told me all my siblings were moving also. It didn't take long to make up my mind and relocate with my family to Georgia.

Fred had already moved to Georgia and started a music company. I sold Clinique Hair Studio to one of the beauticians, packed up and moved to Georgia not knowing whether I'd like living there or not. I had visited Georgia twice, but I never considered moving there and opening a business. Once I arrived in Georgia and learned my way around, I fell in love with it. I lived with Mom in a beautiful two-story house she bought in a city on the outskirts of Atlanta called Lithonia.

My chances to succeed seemed greater in Georgia because black people and their businesses appeared to be on the move, as opposed to those in the Fort Lauderdale and Hallandale area. I felt moving to Atlanta was a good change for me. I decided to go into the hair business with my family so I wouldn't be tied up in running a business by myself and not being able to attend real estate school. The family pulled together and decided to open two hair salons in different locations. We opened Lavon Hair Studio and Glama-Rama Hair Fashion in Decatur, Georgia. Right away, the business started doing well. Glama-Rama had twelve stations. I worked at one station, and we rented out the rest. Lavon Hair Studio was much smaller with only six stations, which we rented out.

I can write another book on my experiences working at Glama-Rama. Never was there a boring atmosphere while working there. Even with bad weather and slow business days, the hot topics women in the salon came up with kept the atmosphere exciting.

Chapter 2

WISHFUL LOVE

*A*s I am standing on a river's bank, billowing clouds are low and dark, and I am looking down at crystal clear water wash up on my bare feet. I gaze out over a wide body of water the size of Lake Erie. The crystal clear water gradually fades to blackness.

I turn left because the image of a man demands my attention. His shadow stands with no distinct features. A small still voice whispers, "Are you not afraid?" The image doesn't frighten me, but I am puzzled about the figures in his hands and his blurry image magically floating six feet in front of me. He's now close enough for me to make out the dozen of white roses in his right hand, and a small storm the shape of a bouquet of roses is spinning like a tornado in his left hand. With wide eyes fixed on the tornado as it spins in his left hand, I blink repeatedly. Each blink seems to take a couple of seconds as my eyelids slowly fall and recede then releases back my sight.

The image stands before me with his right hand extended, offering me the bouquet of white roses. First hesitating then thinking, "What's the harm," I reach to take the white roses. The moment my hand grabs the white roses' stems, the bouquet begins *to spin into a tornado matching the likeness of the tornado in his left hand. The power of this small rotating force proves violently strong until I can feel the thorns rip away at the flesh inside the palm of my hand. The sharp pain apprehends my entire body, causing my hand to snatch away.*

Abruptly, I awake from my sleep panting and breathing hard with my mind spinning in dizziness. The torturing and confusing dream formulated beads of sweat on my forehead. I can almost taste the fear trapped inside my heart and throat. Dazed, I turn my head to see the clock. It read 4 a.m., and I laid in bed sleepless until 7 a.m.—the time to get ready for work.

After about six months, my work time at Glama-Rama was shortened due to enrollment at MLS Real Estate School, located in a small city right outside of Atlanta called Lawrenceville. Going to real estate school in the mornings and working at the salon in the evenings wasn't easy. Through tiredness, I pressed forward to achieve set goals, having no time for a social life or hanging out with friends. However, Tasha and I spoke often over the telephone and visited each other on occasion because she was still in Florida. I was doing well in real estate school but couldn't wait to finish and free up some extra time for myself. A lot of my clients' hair appointments were moved to weekends upon enrolling in school. On weekends, my work schedule was normally from early mornings to late nights, and sometimes I would not leave Glama-Rama until after eleven o'clock at night.

On top of going to school in the morning, our teacher gave out a lot of homework to prepare for tests that were given almost daily. The real estate board exam could not be taken unless we passed all the classes at MLS Real Estate School first. I passed all my classes at MLS and prepared to take the real estate state board exam.

The day after passing the classes at MLS, I walked through the door of Glama-Rama and said, "Everybody, guess what?" A young beautician stationed next to my station named Kim Lewis blurted out, "Girl, you got your real estate license!"

I replied, "Not yet. I passed my classes at MLS and now I can take the state board exam to get my real estate license."

Mrs. Carrie, an older, motherly type beautician added words of encouragement, "That's good, Debra. We're all proud of you. The state exam is not easy, so if you don't pass it the first time, don't be discouraged because most people taking the exam don't pass the first time."

Welcoming Mrs. Carrie's encouraging words but not entertaining the thought of failing the exam the first time around I replied, "Mrs. Carrie, I'm passing that test on the first time around."

A few ladies in the salon smiled and said, "That's it, girl. You can do it."

I waited a week before taking the exam. After work, I went over the former class work. Rumors had it that the exam took at least three hours. Not wanting to take the exam more than one time, I studied at every given opportunity, even while driving to work and during lunch breaks.

A week passed and the time came to take the state exam. I forced myself to retain as much knowledge about real estate as I could, knowing I'd be relieved and didn't have to memorize as much once I passed the exam. I took the test and passed. I was dissatisfied with my low test score, but I was thankful and relieved for not having to take the exam again. Everyone at Glama-Rama was happy for me. Mrs. Carrie hugged me and said, "Debra, I'm proud of you. When I buy my next house, you will be my real estate agent."

Smiling, I replied, "Okay now. I'm holding you to your word." Some in the salon laughed and made funny comments. No one asked, or seemed to care, about my test score. They were happy I passed the first time around.

A little over two years went by and Glama-Rama and Lavon Hair Salon were doing well. One day while I was with a client, the telephone rang and the young receptionist, Connie Murray, answered the call and said, "Debra, come get the telephone. You have a call from Carla."

I ran to pick up the telephone because it had been a while since I heard from Carla. I spoke in the phone, "Hello, Carla. How are you doing, girl?"

Carla was just as excited to hear my voice as I was to hear hers. "Debra, girl, I'm doing fine. I got married and me and my husband are moving to Atlanta in two months."

I said, "That's great, Carla. It'll be nice to spend some time together with you. Why didn't you call to tell me you were getting married?"

Carla answered, "I tried to call you several times, but you are never at home. I called your friend, Tasha, and she gave me your work number."

I replied, "I'm glad you called me at work because you're right——I am hardly ever home. Most of my time is spent at work."

Carla said, "From now on, I'll call you at work."

I said, "You can call me at home, but you'll have to call after 11 o'clock."

Carla asked, "Did Tasha tell you she is thinking about moving to Atlanta also?"

Surprised, I answered, "No. We talked about it, but she never made up her mind to come. I'll probably call her this week and find out what's up. It would be good if we can all hook up in Atlanta because this is a thriving city for women."

Carla and I reminisced about our college days, and she told me all about her wonderful husband named Craig Gooden and their future plans. Craig was an architect and Carla was a realtor. They felt Atlanta was the best place to accommodate both their professions, so they decided to leave California.

The following day after speaking with Carla, I called Tasha and she answered the telephone. "Hello? Hey, Debra. How are you doing?"

I replied, "I'm fine. So when were you going to tell me you are moving to Atlanta?"

She answered, "After I got there. I wanted to surprise you. Carla told you, huh?"

I answered, "Yep."

Tasha said, "Something told me not to say anything. I forgot to tell her not to mention it."

More excited than Tasha about her moving I asked, "So when

47

are you coming?"

Tasha replied, "In about three months, right after the Christmas holidays."

I replied in excitement, "Girl, I can't wait. At least we can hang out together."

Right after Christmas, I was blessed to be in the same town with my closest friends. Carla and Tasha hit it off well and we all enjoyed each other's company. Being married and working as a realtor, Carla didn't get to spend much time with Tasha and I. Tasha had become an excellent hair stylist, so she started working at Lavon Hair Studio; all the stations were rented out at Glama-Rama. After a year, one of the beauticians left Lavon and I moved to work there with Tasha. My clients were very pleased with my work and didn't have a problem changing locations. I especially liked the move for two main reasons: firstly, because I was able to be working side by side with Tasha and secondly, I could get away from Glama-Rama because of the endless gossip.

Lavon was much smaller and the gossiping was not as bad. Some of the girls at Glama-Rama were loud, annoying and unashamed when talking about various subjects. They talked about any and everything. Glama-Rama became like an information center, sometimes having three separate arguments going at one time. One can only imagine how chaotic the atmosphere may have been. I did learn a lot because of the various topics discussed, but the change was much needed. Lavon enabled me to think clearly. There wasn't as much excitement in the air compared to Glama-Rama, but the atmosphere was just right for me.

The days seemed longer, but my head was clearer, giving me

more time to think of my future plans for achieving set goals. Tasha didn't have many clients and at the time I considered it a blessing because she helped with my clients when she was not busy with hers. That allowed me some free time to start concentrating on putting my real estate skills to work.

One day, I had to go downtown to City Hall. When leaving out the building headed for the parking lot, I noticed a guy coming towards me.

Our eyes locked as we looked in each other's face. He really attracted me and as our distance drew nearer, I could no longer maintain my stare so I smiled and tried to look past him. I refocused my attention to his face as he spoke, "Hi, how are you doing?"

In a quick glance, I surveyed him up and down, then responded with a big smile, "I'm fine, thank you." Neither one of us broke our stride as we walked right past each other.

He was tall and handsome, light brown complexion, which complimented his light brown eyes and straight white teeth. We probably were thinking the same thing in passing, "Wow, what a missed opportunity." We both turned to look back at each other at the same time and stared for two seconds. I turned to go to my car and he turned to go into the City Hall building, tripping on the steps because he didn't watch where he was going. I giggled inside as he stumbled to catch his fall.

Once in the car, I fumbled around in my pocketbook hoping he would change his course of direction and walk back outside to at least ask for my telephone number. He looked to be everything I wanted in a man, but there was no way I could work up enough nerves to go back inside City Hall to ask for his telephone number.

After a minute or two of fumbling around in my purse and recognizing he wasn't coming back, I cranked the car engine, put the car in reverse and drove out the parking lot thinking, "Oh well, I guess he wasn't that interested—-another missed opportunity." As I drove back to Lavon, I couldn't get the picture of his face out my mind. To me, he looked better than Denzel Washington. His eyes gave him the edge over Denzel. There was something about his eyes that captivated me and I couldn't wait to tell Tasha about him.

I walked into Lavon and said to Tasha, "Girl, let me tell you about this cute guy I saw at City Hall."

My words blew by Tasha without her giving them a thought, "Yeah, well guess who called?"

Curious, I asked, "Who?"

Tasha acted like she wanted to play cat and mouse with words to hold me in suspense, "Who haven't you heard from since college?"

By the way Tasha acted, I thought she was talking about a man friend, so I answered, "Who? Shawn?"

Tasha sucked her teeth in disappointment because I didn't give the right answer, "Naw…Nikki!"

Surprised, I asked, "Nikki?"

Tasha continued, "Yeah, she called because she heard your name over the radio while advertising the hair salons. She's living here in Atlanta."

I thought, "This is almost unbelievable." Then I asked, "Did she leave her telephone number?"

Tasha answered, "Yeah, I told her Carla also lives here in Atlanta. She wants you to call right away." Tasha handed me the telephone number on a piece of paper and I slipped it in my jean pocket. Tasha asked, "Aren't you going to call? Sounds like she wants to hear from you right away."

I really thought after college I would never see Nikki again. There was no rush to call Nikki because we weren't close like Carla and I. During college, Nikki played to a totally different tune than me. By her being a party animal, I wasn't interested in getting caught up in her fast way of life so I was reluctant to call her. I answered Tasha, "I'm going to call her, but let me tell you about this nice looking guy I saw at City Hall."

Tasha became all ears, "Oh yeah, tell me about him then."

I said, "Well, he's tall and handsome with the most gorgeous eyes a man can have."

Tasha asked, "What's his name?"

Shamefully, I answered, "I don't know."

Tasha asked, "Didn't y'all talk?"

I replied, "No."

Tasha continued with the questions, "Did you exchange phone numbers?"

Embarrassed, I answered Tasha again, "Nope. We just spoke to each other as we passed."

Tasha cut her eyes at me, "So you don't know how to get in touch with him, or if you'll ever see him again?"

I agreed, "Yep…I'm afraid you're right. I was too shy to ask for his phone number and hoped he would ask for mine, but he didn't."

Tasha rolled her eyes at me. "That's smart of you. You probably blew a good thing."

Tasha lectured on, "Debra, you have to learn to be more aggressive with men these days, or else you'll never have anybody. There's a shortage of men and you have to make your move quick."

I replied nonchalantly, "Well, if it's meant for something to happen, I'll see him again one day."

Tasha replied sarcastically, "Yeah, you'll be waiting until you're a hundred years old thinking that way. You've got to make it happen."

Tasha's last comment made sense and gave me something to think about. I walked over to the telephone, took Nikki's telephone number out my pocket and dialed her number.

Chapter 3

TOGETHER AGAIN

Fernando Jenkins and his friends, Wayne Crouch and Michael "Smitty" Smith (two pretty boy player wanna-be's), sit in Fernando's 1996 Saab listening to old school tunes driving east on Interstate 20 headed to Wesley Chapel Road to play basketball. Fernando pulls into the gym's parking lot, and they get out the car dressed in shorts, sneakers and T-shirts ready to play.

Smitty dribbles the basketball as they walk towards the gym door. Smitty says to Fernando and Wayne, "Man, let's go in here and show these boys how to really play basketball."

Wayne replies, "I hope you came to play team ball without thinking you're Michael Jordan."

Smitty can't pass up the opportunity to respond, "You must have forgotten...I have the same first name as Jordan, fool!"

Fernando snickers, "Y'all boys always tripping—neither one of you can play ball for real."

Smitty blasts Fernando, "What! I know you ain't talking 'bout game, 'cause your game is some straight garbage!"

They enter the gym to the smell of sweat and the sound of squeaking gym shoes from guys engaged in an intense basketball game. Wayne sees his friend, Slow, on the basketball court and yells to him, "Hey, Slow. Me and my boys got next! What's the score?"

Slow hollers back, "We need four points and it's over!"

Wayne, Fernando and Smitty sit in the gym bleachers watching the guys on the court while they wait for their turn to play.

Slow's team can't finish off their opponents, and they end up losing the game. Wayne leaves the bleachers and goes onto the court, saying, "Slow, you and your partners have a seat and we'll show you how to take care of business. You guys should have won the game." Wayne, Fernando and Smitty engage in a heated and intense game with the other team, pushing, bucking for position under the basket and giving each other hard fouls.

Ramon, an average black basketball player on the opposite team, dribbles the ball to the basket while Fernando follows closely playing defense. Ramon lays up the ball and it hits the backboard hard then bounces off the rim. Ramon shouts, "Foul!"

Fernando explodes in anger. "Foul! What do you mean, foul! I didn't touch you! You missed the shot!"

Ramon walks to the top of the court and says, "You fouled me, man. You rode me all the way to the basket."

Fernando snaps, "You're a lie! I didn't touch you!"

Fernando holds the basketball as Wayne tries to convince him to give Ramon the ball. "Give him the ball, Fernando, and don't worry about it."

Angrily, Fernando replies, "Naw!! I'm not giving him nothing. This punk is trying to cheat!"

Ramon responds furiously, "Nigger, who are you calling a punk! I'll kick your butt!"

Fernando backs down, turns around and kicks the basketball as hard as he can to the other end of the court, then walks toward the door.

Smitty tries to bring calm to the situation, "Cool out, Fernando. It's just a game. Come on, let's go before we get into something with these guys." Everyone in the gym watched as Smitty retrieves his basketball from the bleachers, leaves out the gym behind Wayne and Fernando, and then they get in the car. Fernando is steaming mad as he starts the engine, then he burns rubber as he spins out the parking lot leaving a trail of smoke behind.

Wayne looks at Fernando and says, "Fernando, you need to chill a little and control your anger. Don't let a game get you all ruffled up."

Fernando frowns at Wayne and shouts,"What! That punk knows I didn't foul him. I didn't touch him."

Wayne replies, "Yeah, but still…"

Fernando interrupts, "But what! That punk tried to cheat us 'cause he didn't want to lose!"

Wayne looks at Fernando's wrinkled face of anger and says, "I understand, but just let it go. You are steaming mad over a game and you look like you wanna kill something."

Fernando responds in frustration, "I do…I wanna kill that nigger. That's why I don't like coming out and being 'round people."

Hesitantly, Smitty speaks, "You can't think like that. You have to come out 'cause you spend too much time alone and keep everything bundled up inside. That's why it's so easy for you to blow your cool and explode."

Fernando rolls his eyes at Smitty and asks, "What are you? A therapist now…"

Smitty answers, "No, I'm just keeping it real."

Fernando responds sarcastically, "Yeah, you're keeping it real alright. If you were keeping it real, you would agree that I didn't foul that punk." Smitty doesn't respond, and for the next 20 minutes they ride home in silence listening to the car radio.

Meanwhile, Nikki sat at her desk when the telephone flashed, alerting her of an incoming call. She answered the telephone, "Hello, Brandon and Weiner Law Office. How may I help you?"

I asked, "May I please speak with Nikki?"

Nikki answered, "Yes, this is she speaking."

Not wanting to keep her in suspense I said, "Hey, Nikki. This is Debra. How are you doing?"

She replied, "I'm fine. It's good to hear your voice. I see you got my message."

I said, "Yeah, girl. How long you been in Atlanta?"

Nikki answered, "About two years. I got married and I have a little girl named Priscilla. I heard Carla lives here in Atlanta also."

I replied, "Yeah, Carla got married and moved here less than two years ago. I talk to her all the time. She's going to be happy to hear you are here in Atlanta."

Nikki said, "Debra, ain't it funny how we all ended up in Atlanta? I guess it was meant to be. We have to hook up. I never thought we'd all be back together so soon. What about you? Have you gotten married yet?"

I answered hesitantly, "No, not yet."

Nikki asked, "What are you waiting for?"

I answered, "I'll let it happen when it happens."

I could hear Nikki's voice change a little because she smiled while replying, "Okay, girl."

Nikki and I talked for over 30 minutes, and we talked of plans to get with the other girls and have lunch the following week. I called everyone and organized the time and place to meet.

I decided that Houston's Restaurant would be the perfect place for dining. Finally, the day had come for the girls' day out.

Tasha and I walked into Houston's Restaurant located by Lenox Mall in Buckhead, an upscale Atlanta community. Houston's was a very classy restaurant that I would so often visit. I always loved to dine there because of the beautiful ambiance.

Carla and Nikki were already at the restaurant and had a table in the back waiting for us. Tasha met Carla months ago, but she had never met Nikki. Tasha heard Carla and I talk about Nikki, and during college, Carla and Nikki often heard me talk about Tasha. They knew Tasha was my best friend.

I introduced Tasha to Nikki. "Nikki, this is my best friend, Tasha I told you about while we were in college."

Nikki greeted Tasha as we embraced each other. "Hello, Tasha. I heard a lot about you," said Nikki.

Tasha smiled and said as we sat down in the booth, "Tell me, Nikki. How do you like Atlanta?"

Nikki answered, "Oh, I love this city. This is the ideal place for me."

I couldn't help but wonder why Nikki liked the city so much

and couldn't resist asking jokingly, "Why do you love the city? Is it because of the men?"

Nikki smiled and answered, "Now, Debra....well, you're kind of right—-at first, but now I've found my dream man."

Nikki looked at Tasha and I then asked, "What are you two waiting on to get married? You'd better hurry and get one of these fine corporate hunks before the women in this city gobble them all up."

I found myself sounding like a tape recorder every time the conversation of marriage came up, "I'm waiting on Mr. Right. I just want a good simple life with a small family."

Carla, in her politeness and shyness, surprised me when she asked Tasha, "What are you waiting for, until you get fifty?"

Everyone smiled and Tasha said, "I've been looking, but all I keep coming up with is a bunch of fake business cards from a lot of fake guys."

I agreed, "She's right. Some of them look good, but they think we are airheads and will not check up on them. I'm just being careful."

Tasha asked, "Nikki, what is your husband's name? Tell us a little about your love."

Nikki was more than happy to tell us about her husband. We saw the excitement formulate on her face as she began to speak, "His name is Melvin Greene. He's from North Carolina and attended the University of Miami on a football scholarship. Put it like this, he's a twin to Al B. Sure. Y'all will get a chance to meet him. He's quiet and sweet. I couldn't ask for a better man."

I complimented Nikki, "You're blessed to find a good man

because there aren't many left. Most of the men here are dead, married, gay, drug and alcohol addicts or HIV positive."

Trying to get the attention off her, Nikki turned and asked Carla, "What about your husband? Tell us about him."

Carla replied shyly while smiling, "Well…what can I say? His name is Craig Gooden. He's smart, good looking and tall. He's what I pictured as a husband and we love each other."

Carla hesitated as though she searched for words to finish describing Craig. I butted in to help her, "Okay, Mrs. Gooden. Go on with your bad self. So what kind of personality does he have? And what kind of work does he do?"

Carla answered, giving me a slight smile for the bailout, "He's a serious man, but he does laugh at times. Our personalities kind of go hand in hand. He has a good job, and he sits on the executive board for Sky Tech Electronics."

Carla stopped talking as the waitress walked to our table and politely interrupted us, "Excuse me. Please forgive me for taking so long. Are you beautiful ladies ready to place your orders?"

We were so excited and engaged in conversation we didn't think about looking at the menus on the table in front of us. I said, "We're sorry. Can you give us five minutes and then we'll be ready to order."

The waitress agreed then left and returned five minutes later. She took our orders and shortly after brought our meals. The food was delicious, leaving us full, satisfied and impressed.

After I finished eating, Tasha and Carla were still eating. I sat back in the booth letting my food settle and thinking about how much Nikki had changed for the better. She looked and acted so mature and professional. I just knew she was going to be a wild child all her life, but it's good being wrong sometimes. I figured married life helped settle her from the previous streak of wildness. Nikki still had a drawing presence and style about her and she knew it; she handled herself well.

As we got up to leave, the guys in the restaurant literally stopped to watch us walk by. Nikki wore a nice business suit. It was tailored to her body, showing every curve. She drew most of the attention, so the rest of us felt invisible and lost in the trail of her presence. Nikki still had that well-defined "drop-dead Coke bottle shape," and guys couldn't help themselves at her passing. The rest of us dressed casually, but nicely.

I glanced down at some of the couples sitting at their tables as we walked by and saw women pinching or slapping their men on the shoulder to stop them from staring at us. Nikki and Carla walked to the door in confidence and contentment, looking straight ahead to make a silent statement that they were not interested or looking for companionship. However, that wasn't the case for Tasha and I. We looked around to see who was looking at us because we were available.

As we walked to our cars along the side of the restaurant, Carla whispered to me, "Debra, are you alright? You look very troubled."

Carla knew me well enough to know something pressed heavy on my mind. I tried to play it off. "I'm fine. I've just got a lot of things on my mind that I have to take care of." I was really worried about Fred because he was recently arrested, but it wasn't the time or place to talk about it.

Carla replied, "You know if you need me for anything, I'm here for you."

Very appreciative of Carla's friendship, I said, "Thank you. I'm okay."

We all got in our cars. Nikki returned back to her job, Carla went home and Tasha and I had hair appointments at Lavon. When we arrived at Lavon, our clients were already there waiting. My client was a middle age woman everyone called Mrs. Mary. Boy, she was a gossip, always coming up with new controversial topics to get the atmosphere stirred up. I hurried and apologized for keeping Mrs. Mary waiting because she always looked for a reason to start some mess.

Mrs. Mary knew a little about everything and not much of anything. Her topic today was whether a woman deserves to be beaten by their man if she messes up or provokes him in some way. It was obvious by the look on some of the ladies' faces in the salon they were in total disagreement with Mrs. Mary's views and opinions on the subject. Mrs. Mary expressed several reasons why a woman needed a good butt kicking from her man. I decided not to get into the conversation because I knew very little about the subject of spousal abuse except for a few times when my sister, Valerie, briefly separated from her ex-husband because he punched her and pushed her around, leaving minor bruises over her body.

The negative vibes and expressions from the other ladies didn't faze Mrs. Mary as she callously explained, "If you knew my brother's wife, you'd see why he kicks her butt and keeps her lips swollen — she's a sassy mouth heifer!"

Ann Lopez, one of the ladies under the hair dryer, looked at Mrs. Mary and said, "That's still no reason for him to beat on her and mess up her face. I don't think there's ever a reason a man should hit or beat on a woman like that. His response should be to leave if things get too heated or out of hand, but never to use such violence on her."

Mrs. Mary rolled her eyes at Ann feeling unmoved and replied, "Yeah, whatever. You can't say nothing because you don't know my sister-in-law."

Everyone in the salon could see the conversation formulating to a heating point. Tasha and I tried to play peacemaker by telling Mrs. Mary and Ann to calm down. They made harsh remarks at each other, and our pleading for peace did no good. The next thing we knew, the two were arguing and cursing at each other because Ann told Mrs. Mary her brother was a spineless coward for beating up on a woman. I gathered Ann hit a nerve because Mrs. Mary took everything Ann said very hard and personal. I thought maybe Ann had been abused or battered by a man. She was so mad and upset that after she and Mrs. Mary calmed down, a tear rolled down the side of her cheek. I saw Ann's hurt, but I couldn't feel or identify with the pain on her face. Somehow during the rest of the day, that whole episode kept replaying in the back of my mind. I kept seeing that same tear fall from her eye.

Mrs. Mary caused a very intense and serious atmosphere in the shop. She looked at Ann and shook her head then walked out the salon. No one knew what to say. We were too afraid to break the silence by saying the wrong thing.

Chapter 4

FAMILY ADDITION

Fernando relaxes on the couch in his poorly furnished and decorated two bedroom apartment, listening to Anita Baker's CD on his cheap home center stereo system. There's a knock on the door and he stands up, turns down the stereo, walks to the door and looks through the door's peephole. He sees Smitty on the other side then opens the door to let him in. Fernando says, "What's up, Smitty? Where ya been?"

Smitty lightly rubs his hand on his face and replies, "I just came from the barbershop."

Fernando looks at Smitty's fresh haircut and says, "Okay, I see your barber hooked you up."

Smitty smiles, "I came over to tell you about a birthday party tomorrow night. My cousin, Derrick, got us three invitations to a party. I'm going to pick them up today. So gear up and get ready for tomorrow night because it's showtime, player."

Fernando smiles while at the same time nodding his head side to side in refusal, "I'm sorry, man. I'm not up for partying or going out. You know how I do it. I'm chilling right here in my pad—alone!"

Smitty momentarily looks at Fernando as he refuses to take no for an answer then begs, "Come on, Fernando. You have to go. I've already got your invitation. Besides, you haven't been any-where in four months."

Fernando walks to the stereo center to turn off the stereo and turns on the television. He turns around and says to Smitty, "I'm cool and content right here by myself."

Smitty continues to beg, "Fernando, listen to me. You have to hang out with the guys sometimes. I already told Wayne, and he's looking forward to us going to the party together."

Smitty sees the uninterested expression on Fernando's face, but refuses to lose the battle, "We can't miss this party. I heard Atlanta's finest are going to be there."

Fernando walks over to the couch, sits down and asks, "How many times do you want me to tell you I don't want to go? I don't like being around people that much. You see what happened the last time we went to play ball. Something always happens."

Convincingly as he can, Smitty says, "Fernando, this is a pri-vate party at the Hilton Ballroom with a high class crowd. I heard Monica and Sonya will be there."

Fernando raises an eyebrow, "Sonya? Stop lying."

Smitty smiles, knowing he's gotten Fernando hooked, "I ain't lying. Derrick told me Sonya and Monica will be at the party."

Fernando nods his head up and down with a sinister smile, "Man, Sonya is the finest broad in Atlanta. I'd sho' like to knock her off."

Smitty rubs it in as he sees the lust in Fernando's eyes while he paused thinking about Sonya, "Fernando, you'll do good if you can get either one of those chicks. What you say? Are you coming to the party?"

Fernando answers with a scheming facial expression, "Yeah, it's worth going just to get a glimpse of Sonya. Don't get me wrong. I don't want her for my lady; she's just a high class whore who happens to be super-duper fine. I just want to do some freaky things to her."

Smitty looks at his watch and says, "Looks like the dark side is coming out. You amaze me how sometimes you can come to life. Don't let me find out you got two personalities. So are we on for tomorrow night?"

Fernando nods his head in confirmation, and Smitty says, "I'm going to go get some fresh gear from Boogie's Clothing Store."

Smitty smiles, waiting for a response from Fernando, but he doesn't receive one. Smitty says, "You might as well come. You might see something you like."

Fernando accepts the offer and says, "Okay, you've convinced me. I guess I'll have to go all the way out and dress to impress."

Smitty replies, "That's my boy. We have to get you to the barber to tighten up your wig."

Fernando and Smitty leave out the apartment, get in Fernando's car and head for the barbershop and clothing store.

Later that day, my mind drifted to Carla because several weeks had passed since I last talked with her. I called and called but wasn't able to get in touch with her. I left messages on her answering machine, but she never called back. This wasn't like

Carla. I figured if something was wrong, she would've called me by now. So I decided not to hunt her down because when she gets ready to call, she will.

Returning home that night feeling sick, tired and worn, all I could do was take a hot bath then go straight to bed. The telephones were turned down low to keep from disturbing my sleep. At times, sleeping was an escape for me because of my constant dreaming. Sometimes I awoke in the mornings from dreaming all night, and then lay in bed thinking and trying to figure out the dreams. I enjoyed dreaming, and for some reason, I felt the dreams were always trying to tell me something. Yet, I was never able to interpret them.

After sleeping hard through the night, I awoke the next morning feeling much better than the day before. My body still felt weak and my nose was a little runny, but my sickness wasn't too serious. I didn't have much time to lie in bed and meditate because I had to meet Mom at Glama-Rama at 8 a.m.

I looked at the clock on the night stand. The time read 7:20 a.m. I had to lay in bed for at least five minutes to reflect back on my dream. Sometimes, there were series of dreams I had at night, but mostly only the last dream seemed clear and complete enough to remember or explain.

I walked into Glama-Rama at 8:05 a.m. Mrs. Carrie and a few beauticians had clients sitting in their chairs. I greeted everyone and walked back to the office where Mom sat behind the desk shuffling papers around and writing out checks to pay bills. Once in the office, I closed the door behind me and greeted Mom, "Good morning, Mommie."

She looked up from the desk, returning the salutation. "Good morning, honey. How are you doing?"

Though I had a mountain of things to do, but not wanting to put any problems on Mom, I answered, "I'm doing alright — just a few little things to take care of today." I paused for a moment because my dream pressed heavy on my mind and I said, "Mommie, I had a strange dream."

Always with a listening ear and ready to help, Mom said, "Tell me about your dream."

Anxious to hear what Mom had to say, I replied, "The dream is kinda short. In the dream was an old man with a dark complexion wearing a pair of shorts with no shirt on, barefooted and carrying two old suitcases full of cheap clothes. He walked north on Highway 1-75 headed for Georgia. I walked along beside him and tried talking with him, but he remained quiet. I asked him questions like, 'Where are you going? Where are you from? Why don't you have on a shirt or shoes?' He turned his head to look at me as we continued walking. I saw sadness in his face while his eyes begged for help. To the side of us were orange groves that appeared all the way until we walked past a huge road sign that read, 'Welcome to the state of Georgia.' That's all I can remember."

Mom sat behind the desk in deep thought for several seconds and said, "Looks like we may have a relative coming to visit us from Florida who may be in need of help, a place to stay and a new start on life."

I listened to Mom explain the dream, and as she continued talking, the dream actually started making sense to me. I didn't give the dream much thought after that, but went about completing the billion plus things I had to do that day.

One week later, Mom called me on the telephone and asked me to stop by her house because her uncle, Ezekiel Johnson, was at the house. Mom and all the family called him Uncle Zek. Mom told me he lived in Miami and came to stay with her and that he would be helping out at the salons. Just like Mom interpreted my dream, Uncle Zek came from Florida and was in need. He was the nicest guy you could ever meet. He had a dark complexion, was very bubbly in character with a deep Bahamian accent, loved whiskey and had a million funny jokes to tell. And, boy, when he got a little tipsy from alcohol, he used to get all of us confused. For example, several months after his arrival, while we were at the dinner table, Uncle Zek said, "Hey, did you all hear about your Mom's friend, Ms. Pat, from up the street?"

And I said, "No? What about her, Uncle Zek?"

He replied, "Well, Pat told me that she had gonorrhea really bad."

We then all replied to him at the same time and in shock, "Gonorrhea?"

And I said, "Do you mean the STD?"

Then he answered, "No, not that. The loose bowels…I mean diarrhea!"

So, you can only imagine how crazy Uncle Zek was. He came to the salons and helped out by keeping both places clean. He helped run errands, bought lunch for everybody and did anything else that needed to be done. He really made things easy for me. He was a real blessing. Everyone fell in love with him and he kept us laughing. At Mom's house, he constantly worked, keeping the entire house clean, cooking excellent Bahamian meals, cutting the grass and doing whatever else needed to be done around the house. It was as if Uncle Zek came and took a big load off Mom's and my shoulders and placed them on his shoulders.

Uncle Zek lived with us once before when I was very little. He stayed with us briefly. He came from the Bahamas to live with us after being brutally assaulted by the Bahamian authorities because they thought he murdered his wife's lover. They later found out Uncle Zek was innocent because the real killer turned himself in. I guess the killer's conscious ate away at him.

Uncle Zek told us how they tortured him by putting his testicles in a vice then squeezing them until they were swollen to the size of softballs. The Bahamian authorities were trying to make Uncle Zek confess to the murder, but he refused. He said they beat him unconscious, blackening both his eyes, swelling his lips and face and knocking out six of his front teeth.

Mom helped make arrangements to have him shipped to America and live with us. When he arrived in America, he was still in bad shape. Mom had to nurse, feed, bathe and clothe him. Uncle Zek recovered and vowed he would never return or set foot on Bahamian soil as long as he lived because of what they did to him. If any of his family wanted to see him, they would have to come to America. He kept his word until the day he died. He divorced his wife, left all his property to his children and never looked back.

When Uncle Zek came to live and work with Mom, she paid him well and he didn't want for anything. He made enough money to live on his own, but decided to stay with Mom. He enjoyed his new life in Atlanta. Two months after Uncle Zek arrived in Atlanta, he was at Lavon's painting the bathroom. The telephone rang and he ran from the bathroom to answer it before any of us could get to it. He handed me the telephone and said, "Debra, Carla is on the phone."

I reached for the telephone and thanked him. I spoke in the telephone, "Hello, Carla. How are you doing, girl? What happened to you?"

I heard a little sadness in Carla's voice as she spoke, "I'm alright. I flew out to California to stay with my parents for a while because Craig and I were having a few problems."

I asked, "Are you still having problems? Can I do anything to help?"

Carla answered, "No, thank you. I'm fine now. It wasn't serious. We worked things out and I'm coming back to Atlanta in a couple of days. I just needed some time alone. Forgive me for not calling sooner. I know you were probably worried about me."

I replied, "Yeah, you're right. I worried, but I'm relieved now that I know you're alright."

Carla and I talked for several minutes, and she agreed to call me when she got back home in Atlanta.

Chapter 5

FALLING IN LOVE

Fernando, Wayne and Smitty sat in Fernando's apartment drinking beer and smoking marijuana. Fernando sat on the couch with his legs kicked out in front of him and his head hung back enjoying his high. Wayne looked at Smitty and said, "Well, kid. Tonight is the night. I can't wait to see all them fine honies."

Smitty replied with a slur, "Yeah, them ladies probably stacked up with paper...some real high class broads."

Wayne said, "Man, it would be a double whammy if we get a girl to sex, and she got big money."

Smitty looked at Fernando and said, "Fernando ain't thinking 'bout nothing but Sonya. I hope you pull her. Maybe she can jump start your dead batteries."

Wayne burst out laughing and Smitty smiled, looking at Fernando as he sat still with his head cocked back on the couch. Thirty seconds later, Fernando slowly raised his head from the couch to respond as though the beer and marijuana caused his brain a delayed reaction. With his eyes half open, Fernando said, "Wayne, forget about finding a lady with big money. Find a job..." They all erupted in laughter.

Everyone lounged around the apartment all day and night until the time came to get ready for the party. Wayne and Smitty brought their clothes to Fernando's apartment so they could get ready and go to the party together. They were dressed up looking like a million bucks although they couldn't scrape up two hundred dollars between the three of them. Fernando was the only one with a half decent job, but most of his money was spent on rent and on his car, having barely enough money left over to buy groceries. Wayne and Smitty refused to get decent jobs. They hustled by helping boosters sell stolen clothes and merchandise, for which they got a percentage from the profits. That explained why they dressed nice in such expensive clothes—-they were stolen!

Fernando and Smitty had gone to Boogie's Clothing Store to see what they wanted, then called their booster friends, and had them steal the clothes. In return, they gave them a little money for the job. Most of the boosters were drug addicts and were just out to get enough money to satisfy getting high throughout the night.

They got dressed then headed for downtown Atlanta. Fernando seemed unexcited as he pulled into the Hilton Hotel's parking lot. Smitty and Wayne were in the car juiced up, bumping and nodding their heads to the song, "More Bounce to the Ounce," by Roger Troutman. From the back seat, Wayne reached and touched Fernando's shoulder and said excitedly, "Loosen up, pretty boy. It's on — it's time to get hyped."

Contained and standing on a lake of crystal clear water, I lower my head to see fish swimming beneath my feet. Raising my head, I glare out over the river. It is the same place in my previous dream with the exception of the surroundings, which appear much smaller than the dream before.

The water underneath my feet creates a shade of two different colors. Half the water is clear as glass and the other half is black as tar. I think, "Why the sudden change?" Out of the blue, there stands that man again. This time, both hands are hidden behind his back and now I can make out the black and white tuxedo he is wearing, but still his face is unrecognizable. With a stone dark face, he stares at me and I stare back intensely. His obscure, beady eyes light up in the deep dark setting of his eye sockets. His eyes flash from hazel to light hazel, from blue to light blue, then from brown to light brown, and instantly the flashing eyes stop. I think, "How tantalizing are those light brown eyes!"

The moment my thoughts end, it seems as if the man knew my thinking, and he smiles as my shyness returns a smile creased across my teeth. The man pulls two dozen red roses from behind his back. Each hand held a dozen flawless roses. The roses radiate with a sparkling red glow. I think, "How lovely are those red roses." Before my thoughts can finish, the man's smile disappears and his face disfigures in cruel anger. With his head hung down, gaseous smoke seeps from the pores and cracks of his skin. He squeezes both hands tightly around the thorns. The thorns on the rose stems pierce through his hands. The pain doesn't seem to faze him. With both arms extended in the air as though victory is smelled and tasted in the heat of battle, I watch blood run from two trembling hands and down both his arms. I think, "What have I done to make him so angry?" Anticipating a reaction at

the end of my thoughts, I stare at the roses in his hands and notice
blood sweating from the rose pedals and stems. Slowly raising his
head with deep black beady eyes, he peered at me. His cold stare
was evil and chilling. It cuts pain into my soul, releasing a fear
inside of me that feels almost impossible for one to know.

I trembled and shivered in a cold sweat as my eyes popped open. I lied still in bed for a moment with damp sheets underneath me. I peeped at the clock, and it read 8 a.m. I was late. I jumped up, got dressed fast, and started on my way. Once I arrived at the salon, I worked straight through the day. I finished styling my last client's hair at 9 p.m. I then rushed home to get ready for a private birthday party Nikki asked me and Tasha to attend. The birthday party was for Douglas Newkirk, who is Nikki's husband's best friend. Douglas is a very prosperous black male in his late 30s. He works as a home developer.

Carla made it back to Atlanta, and Nikki invited her and Craig to the birthday party. They accepted the invitation, and I looked forward to seeing Carla because I missed seeing and talking to her.

Though I was dead tired, I needed the night out to have some kind of fun because, for the last two months, I practically worked myself to death. My back hurt and feet ached from the constant standing in the salon. It was time to get out and get some fresh air. Tasha and I talked about going out and possibly getting some kind of male companionship into our lives. Because we worked so much, there wasn't a lot of time for anything else. Being alone bothered me a little. At times, I felt lonely and thought it would

74

be good if I had a decent man to spend some time with.

After closing the hair salon and dropping Uncle Zek off at home, I drove home and ran hot water in the tub to relax for thirty minutes and took a bath. Relaxing in the hot water was just what I needed for rejuvenation. After getting out the tub and drying off, I felt refreshed. I walked to the closet to figure out what to wear. My closet was laced with nice outfits, but the hardest thing was deciding what to wear.

After searching through clothes for five minutes, I pulled a black Liz Claiborne short dress from the closet rack. The dress had an open V-shape low cut style. Fendi was the fashion design in style at the time, and I bought the six hundred dollar matching purse and shoes set to go with the dress.

Tasha did a wonderful job on my hair, and earlier that day during lunch break, I polished my nails. That night, I dressed to kill. After putting on makeup and getting dressed, I drove fifteen minutes to Roswell, Georgia to pick up Tasha at her condominium. She lived alone in a nice quiet upper middle class neighborhood. Her condo was nicely furnished and decorated. She worked hard, saved money and spent it wisely. We both worked hard and deserved nice things.

When Tasha answered the door dressed in a beautiful white two piece skirt outfit with light goldish lacing, she looked stunning. To the guys, she was going to be a knockout. Tasha stood several feet inside the doorway, turned around and asked, "How do I look?"

Smiling, I answered, "That skirt is way too short—just kidding. You look great, and I love your outfit."

Tasha said, "I have to admit that's a beautiful dress you're wearing—a little provocative, but nice. The women tonight will be very envious." We laughed.

Walking into Tasha's condo gave me a warm and serene feeling. The living room was set in the color of soft eggshell white. The carpet was slightly darker than the bone-white couch, and the big fireplace was carved in off-white keystone. The living room and dining room were decorated in modern elegance with soft blues complimenting the back room, which was laid out in contemporary furnishings and styles. Tasha really impressed me with her good taste in decorating. Mom made all the drapes for the windows, and the creamy light beige swags trimmed in bronze-colored tassels set off the front portion of the condo.

Luther Vandross' song played softly on the stereo while Tasha hurried around in the back room getting ready, putting finishing beauty touches to her makeup. We were dressed and ready to steal the city's heart away in our killer outfits.

We arrived at the downtown Atlanta Hilton about 11 p.m. The parking area was filled with Mercedes Benz, Porches, Rolls Royces and other nice expensive cars driven by those attending Douglas' birthday party. Good looking men and women filled the ballroom, walking around in classy attire carrying wine glasses in their hands. I was excited about being there. It looked like all Atlanta's wealthiest were there. The crowd was racially mixed, and everyone appeared to know each other. The mood in the ballroom was pleasant and the air was filled with clashing perfumes and colognes. Overhead, big beautiful, dimly lit crystal chandeliers cast a soft glow on everything below, giving the ballroom a softening cozy feel. There were expensive couches and chairs the replica of Louis XV furniture. Everything looked expensive from the ceiling, walls, furniture to the carpet.

Tasha and I walked around looking for familiar faces, but we saw none as we caught the looks and stares from others around us. The ballroom was conveniently sectioned off to accommodate couples and groups. We looked for an untaken section so we could park for the night. Spotting a table, we started walking towards it when Carla and Craig walked up behind us. I turned at the sound of Carla's voice, "Hey, Debra and Tasha."

Excited, I said, "Carla!" We all hugged each other.

Craig stood smiling as Carla said, "Follow us; we already have a reserved section." As we walked through the crowd and closer to our table, I saw Nikki and Melvin sitting at the table talking. We walked to the table and greeted Nikki and Melvin. As we were about to sit down, Melvin asked us to follow him so we could find and meet his best friend, Douglas, to wish him happy birthday. When we found Douglas, he was dressed very nicely, surrounded by friends and his new girlfriend, Donna, who hung on his arm like a Christmas ornament. There was no question she wanted everyone to know Douglas was taken and all hers. Donna was highly attractive, but somewhat dingy, yet smart enough not to let Douglas out of her sight. She guarded Douglas like a territorial animal on alert for anyone intruding on her site. She didn't have to say anything in guarding over Douglas because her slight frown, rolling eyes and head gestures spoke loud enough. I couldn't blame her because there were a lot of attractive and wealthy females in the ballroom who would love to have Douglas as their man, including myself. Douglas had the whole package: he was handsome, polite, charming, and rich.

After saying happy birthday and meeting Douglas for the first time, we all retreated to our table. We all sat watching couples dance. I didn't feel like dancing because I was hungry. Plus my feet were tired from standing in the salon all day.

We had a choice to wait on a waiter to come to our table and serve us food from the large feeding area, or we could go to the serving line and fix a plate of food ourselves. Tasha and I decided to help ourselves instead of waiting because we were starving. When we got to the food area, we couldn't believe our eyes. They had the best of everything: carefully prepared meats, pastries, wines and a big birthday cake already cut, but I could still make out the writing on the cake which said, "Happy 35th Birthday. We love you, Douglas."

My eyes were bigger than my stomach because I hadn't eaten all day. I put a little of everything on my plate, knowing I couldn't eat all that food in one setting. We took our food back to the table and chowed down. The food was absolutely delicious. When I finished eating, I sat at the table satisfied, and I watched everyone enjoy themselves. Everyone had a bottle of Dom Perignon wine at their tables, but I was full and couldn't take a sip of anything because my stomach would probably burst open.

The bar was set up in case someone desired stronger drinks. From my table, I watched partygoers — men and women alike — refuse to leave the bar as they drank glass after glass until they were flared up, drunk and talking loud.

I saw three nicely dressed young black men walk to the bar.

They looked around as though they were out of place and stumbled in the ballroom by accident. It was obvious they had a right to be at the party because the security at the door was very strict about letting people in. Without an invitation, it was almost impossible to get into the party.

At a distance, one of the guys standing at the bar looked familiar, but I couldn't quite make him out. On the sly, I kept staring because his face wouldn't let my spirit settle until I figured out from where I knew him.

Fernando, Wayne and Smitty stood at the bar ordering drinks. Smitty twirled around looking at every short skirt that passed, trying to capture and record their images in the back of his mind. He said to Fernando and Wayne, "Man, look at all these fine honies in here. This can't be real."

Wayne replied, "You're right. I'm just wondering where all these ladies been hiding because as fine and pretty as they are, I'm supposed to know them."

Fernando stood poised and more in control. He looked around and agreed with his friends that there were a lot of beautiful and classy looking women, but his mind was locked on seeing one woman as he asked, "Does anyone see Sonya?"

Smitty frowned, looked at Fernando and snarled comically, "What? Man, the hell with Sonya and Monica. Look at all these bad, super-fine chicks in here. It should be against the law to have this many fine women in one place!"

Wayne said, "Come on y'all, let's walk around and check things out."

Fernando insisted on staying at the bar, "I'm cool right here

79

enjoying the scene."

Wayne looked at Fernando and said, "Alright, do what you feel, but I'm out — Audi 5,000." Wayne and Smitty walked away from the bar, disappearing into the crowd leaving Fernando standing by himself.

Sitting at the table, I continued glancing at the familiar looking young man until it came to me where I first saw him. I nudged Tasha and said, "Tasha, Tasha."

Tasha sat stuffing her face with food and replied with her mouth full, "What, Debra?"

Excitedly, I said, "That's the guy, the one I told you about."

Tasha looked confused, having no idea what guy I was talking about, "What guy? What are you talking about, Debra?"

I answered, "The guy I told you about who I met one day coming out of City Hall."

Tasha remembered, "Oh, the guy whose name you didn't know."

I smiled and said, "Yeah, that guy."

Tasha moved her head side to side like a cobra searching the crowd to see him and asked, "Which one is he?"

Not trying to draw any attention to us, I answered, "The guy at the bar with the nice blue shirt and black pants."

Tasha smiled and said, "Uh, he is cute."

I turned away from facing him so he couldn't see Tasha and I acting like two blushing teenage girls. He didn't see me. I became nervous and asked Tasha, "What should I do? Should I go say something to him?"

Tasha quickly advised me as though she was some kind of

expert in the field of initial introductions, "No, girl. You don't want to make the first move. You definitely don't want him to think you are desperate or easy. Make him work."

Anxiously, I interrupted, "So what should I do?"

The young man stood leaning on the corner of the bar, sipping on a glass of Hennessy and Coke. He appeared content just looking around while his body language showed that he didn't know a soul at the party except the people he came with. Tasha had fun thinking of ways to manipulate the situation for us to meet, "Debra, here is what you do. Pretend you have to use the restroom. When you walk towards him, look in his face until he makes eye contact with you. Then, look away and keep walking past him as though you have no idea who he is."

Puzzled, I asked, "What am I supposed…"

Tasha cut me off, "Just listen, Debra."

I said, "Alright, go ahead. I'm listening."

Tasha continued, "Okay, this is what you do—-walk by him. When you pass, if he remembers your face, he would start thinking of where he saw you. Stay in the restroom for about seven minutes to give him some time to think of what he will say to you—-men can be slow and retarded at times so we have to help the situation without them knowing it." I couldn't help but laugh because I didn't know Tasha was so clever.

Nikki looked across the table at us with a suspicious grin knowing we were up to something. I asked Tasha, "Girl, where did you learn all this?"

Tasha smiled and answered, "Don't worry about that, just do like I tell you." I agreed to play along with Tasha's little scheme.

She asked, "Are you ready?"

Nervously, I answered, "Yeah, but what if it don't work?"

Tasha replied, "Trust me, it'll work. You know women do things differently from men. Besides, when he sees you walk back past him in your sexy black dress, that fool will be hooked, and he will remember you or come up with something to approach you."

Tasha and I giggled like two leprechauns after doing something devious. I stood up, fixed my dress by pulling it down a bit, then I did exactly what Tasha planned. As I walked towards the bar looking into the young man's face, it felt like reliving the day we first made eye contact at City Hall. There's no way he couldn't remember me once he saw me. As soon as he looked at me and made eye contact, I looked away and passed him by inches. I thought, "The games women sometimes play…I guess it's innocent fun." I smiled inside, sensing his whole body turn to look at me as I passed by him. I headed straight for the ladies room and timed myself while fooling around in the mirror, then walked out the bathroom seven minutes later. I took the same route back to the table, but when I approached the bar where the young man stood, he was gone! So much for Tasha's clever plan.

Reaching the table and sitting down, I said to Tasha, "He left…"

Tasha whispered, "Yeah, I watched him leave, but believe me, he got a good look at you when you passed by him. Just wait. If I know men, he'll come sniffing around before the night is over."

Tasha was right. Thirty minutes later, the young man walked

to our table and said to me, "Excuse me. Would you like to dance?"

Forgetting all about my tired feet, I accepted, "Sure. Why not? I would love to dance."

He took me by the hand, leading me to the dance floor. Glancing back briefly, Tasha winked her eye at me with a sinister half smile as to say, "I told you so." Seconds later, I saw Tasha being led to the dance floor by a handsome young man.

There I stood face to face on the dance floor looking at this gorgeous man and getting ready to step into his arms to slow dance to a love song by an R&B group called After 7. Somehow in my heart, I felt we would meet again. He whispered in my ear and asked, "So what is your name?"

I whispered, "Debra Williamson. And your name is?"

I felt the warmth of his breath down my neck as he softly answered, "Fernando Jenkins. Didn't I see you a while back at City Hall?"

I paused from dancing, pulled halfway out his arms, looked in his face and said, "Yeah, that's where I remember you from...City Hall."

Fernando replied, "I remember that day well and wondered if I would ever see you again."

Fernando and I danced to three rounds of slow songs, and it felt as though I melted in his arms. Everything felt so right. After slow dancing, we talked and exchanged telephone numbers and agreed to go out for dinner at a later date. I introduced Fernando to Tasha and everyone at our table.

Afterward, Fernando left and Tasha and I sat talking about

every detail of my short time together with him. The night grew long, and slowly the people at the party started leaving. Everyone at the party seemed to enjoy themselves. Everyone at our table decided to leave together. We found Douglas, thanked him for a wonderful time and said goodbye.

Passing through the hotel lobby on the way out to the parking lot, I saw Fernando and his two friends standing by the telephone at the other end of the lobby. It was obvious Fernando said something to his friends about me because they stared at me with big smiles on their faces. Fernando waved at me and put his hand at his ear in the shape of a make believe telephone and moved his lips deliberately without sound to say, "I'll call you." I nodded my head to let him know I understood and smiled as I walked out the hotel front door.

Meeting Fernando put a spark in my life. My days seemed a lot brighter. Spending time together with him made all the difference in the world for me. I was lonely and he was like the answer to my prayers. We fell in love and everything I did from then on was to please Fernando until I lost focus of my own plans and goals. I didn't fret because he was the perfect gentleman and boyfriend.

Excited about our new relationship, I went out the way to decorate my house to impress him. Mom made draperies for the entire house. The drapes in the dining room and living room were light blue and light mauve colored with bone-white silk sheers laid against white and soft rosy American silk wallpaper. The living room was my favorite. It was the first thing you saw stepping through the front door, so I wanted to make a good first impression. The living room furniture was big, covered in fine ultra-suede material. A beautiful handmade marble wall unit in the shape of ancient Roman pillars with thick glass shelves took up one section of the living room wall. The entire front portion of the house had the old world look mixed with a little modern and contemporary flavor. Overhead in the living room, I installed an expensive crystal and gem stone chandelier.

I had to slow down on spending because I tapped into my emergency funds. I made it a priority to replace the emergency funds as soon as possible. I needed to fix up my house anyway, so the money was well spent.

Fernando really liked my house and complimented me on the decorations. He was so kind, loving and sweet. His concern for my feelings and happiness impressed me the most. We introduced each other to our families and started spending our free time together.

A year later, we dined at a restaurant in Buckhead called Bones, and Fernando proposed to me. He totally caught me off guard when he pulled an engagement ring out his pocket, knelt down on one knee in front of me while surrounded by a bunch of strangers in the restaurant and asked, "Debra, baby. Would you marry me?"

Elated and overjoyed, I became speechless for several seconds then answered, "Yes—oh yes. I'd love to marry you and become Mrs. Jenkins."

Fernando smiled, kissed me and slipped a beautiful 1 ½ carat diamond on my finger. He looked at me and said, "I guess anywhere from a year to two years we can tie the knot."

I thought, "A year or two is kind of a long time," so I asked, "Why do you want to wait that long?" At that time we had been dating for over a year.

With a serious facial expression, he answered, "To be truthful, right now I'm not in the position to offer you a big wedding. Shucks, I don't even have a house to move you in when we get married. I figured I'll save some money in a year or two and then I'll be able to offer you some of the things a husband should offer his wife."

Fernando's honesty captured me, and if that was keeping us from getting married sooner, we didn't have a problem. Being head over hills in love, I said to Fernando, "Baby, listen to me. I have a house and everything we need. When we get married, everything I have is yours. We'll move in my house together and any plans you want to make from there, you are free to make. That way, you can take your time and not be under any kind of pressure."

Fernando looked at me with those beautiful brown eyes and said, "Thanks so much, Debra. I promise you I'm going to make you the happiest woman in the world and try to give you everything your heart desires."

With love-filled eyes, I replied, "I'm already the happiest woman in the world. As long as I have you, I'm fine." We kissed each other then finished eating our dinner. I couldn't have dreamed of a more lovely or perfect night together.

Marrying Fernando would really put my heart and spirit at ease because all the time we were seeing each other and having sex, I stayed under heavy conviction. Though I wasn't a devoted

Christian, I still knew it was wrong to have premarital sex. Every time Fernando and I finished having sex, I laid in bed and pictured going to church as a young girl and the preacher standing in the pulpit preaching how morally wrong it was to have premarital sex and live with a mate you were not married to. He spoke strongly against shacking (living and having sex with a mate while unmarried.) Even though I lived in sin, there was always a part of me that was conscious of God, and it made me want to please Him. These were things in my heart I never shared with Fernando. Many times, I wanted to say something to him about my feelings and the condition of my heart, but I didn't, fearing it might drive him away from me. I loved him so much, and him asking to marry me was the perfect antidote to erase the immoral heaviness lingering in my heart.

The next day, I spent the greater part of the morning running errands and picking up hair supplies, which had to be distributed between Glama-Rama and Lavon. I decided to drop off supplies to Glama-Rama first. Driving into the parking lot of Glama-Rama, I spotted Mrs. Mary's car. Seeing her car explained why I hadn't seen her in a long time at Lavon. She probably was too ashamed or embarrassed to face Ann or show her face back at Lavon because of all the commotion she caused the last time she was there.

Just as I imagined, when I walked into Glama-Rama, Mrs. Mary's mouth was in full gear, and dead center of the conversation. Kim saw me first as I walked through the door and spoke, "Hey, Debra."

I greeted everyone at once, "Hello, how's everybody doing?"

Everyone briefly stopped talking to return my greetings then went right back talking. Whatever they were talking about must have been very interesting because the mood in the salon was exciting and spicy. Everyone's face carried the expression of interest. Mrs. Mary looked at Mrs. Carrie and said, "Girl, you know that sorry husband of mine ain't touched me in two months. He must got an ole' hoochie momma on the side giving him sex, but he's terribly mistaken if he thinks I'm just going to sit back and not get mine. I gotta have some loving too."

Some of the ladies laughed. Maxine, the lady sitting in Kim's chair, said, "Mrs. Mary, I don't know which one of our situations is worse. My husband wants sex too much. I be like, "Damn, man. Ain't you had enough?" Three o'clock in the morning there he goes trying to hunch up on something, knowing I have to go to work early in the morning. Soon as I get home from work, I can't put my bags down good without him calling me to the bedroom—butt naked wanting to have sex. I think that fool is trying to kill me or screw his own brains out."

Everyone burst out in laughter. Mrs. Carrie interrupted, "I guess y'all can say I'm in the middle 'cause my husband gives it to me once a week, or whenever he feels like it. Forget about it if he gets mad. He acts like a little kid with a toy who doesn't want anyone else to play with it except him."

Mrs. Mary said, "Married life can be a trip sometimes, but I refuse to be anybody's doormat."

Mrs. Carrie replied, "Marriage has its ups and downs, its advantages and disadvantages. There've been times when I said to myself, 'Dog, I got to wake up to the same ole' man everyday.'

I've learned that you have to love each other beyond the bedroom because eventually the sex will begin to grow old. It's unimaginable to think of a relationship keeping the same excitement and flavor every year matching the first year of a marriage."

One of the ladies named Faye entered the conversation shyly, "Excuse me. I don't mean to butt in your conversation, but I'm a Christian and I've been married for fifteen years, and my relationship with my husband is just as exciting now as the first day we got married. The key to a successful marriage is both mates centering their relationship on Jesus Christ and He will keep your relationship alive, exciting and active."

It was easy to see by the facial expressions that Mrs. Mary and some of the other ladies weren't interested in Faye's marital advice. They mumbled in a sense of disbelief, "Yeah…" as they brushed Faye off. Even though I held my peace and didn't say anything, the conversation really had me thinking about marriage. At first I planned to break the news to everyone about my engagement to Fernando, but after hearing their conversation about marriage, I decided now wasn't the time. I found myself purposely hiding my hand so no one could see the engagement ring on my finger. I was almost at the point of rethinking my decision of getting married, but Faye's advice helped reinforce my thinking back to getting married. No one wanted to hear what Faye had to say, but she was the only one who seemed to have an answer to the problem while all the other women did was speak about the problem.

Kim hesitantly entered the conversation, "Well, all I can say is that all of you are in a better situation than I am. I'm probably the youngest person in here, but I haven't been touched by a man in over a year and a half. At least y'all are gettin' some."

Mrs. Mary jokingly poked out her lips and said, "Poor child…" Everyone in the salon burst out in laughter. Kim was trying to hold on and be strong, but I saw loneliness eating away at her like a cancer. I once knew the feeling of loneliness, and I wanted my brother out of jail more than Kim did. I understand what Kim went through, and I felt sorry for her because she changed after Fred got locked up. For a woman in love, she always looked sad. Kim became a living example of the phrase, "bittersweet love." She used to be bubbly and talkative, but now she was quiet and withdrawn. I could tell her love for Fred was real and not superficial. I just wondered how long she could hold on in the event Fred didn't get out of prison in the near future. Fred's lawyer filed appeals, and that hope kept us all holding on for a favorable outcome.

The time came for me to leave Glama-Rama, and I was glad to be getting outside to some fresh air because the strong hair chemicals and constant noise was about to give me a headache. I said goodbye to everyone and left out of Glama-Rama to take the rest of the hair supplies to Lavon. Walking out the salon, I walked several yards down the store's sidewalk headed for my car and saw a woman walking towards me dressed in a black flowing cape with her head hung downward. I didn't take much notice to her until she passed by me, and I felt the strong slow dragging wind of her warm presence. Something was strange about this woman, and the outfit she wore seemed ancient and from another time in history. I turned to look at her, and at the same time she turned to look at me. What I saw caused me to freeze in paralyzing terror with my mouth wide open. She absolutely scared the daylights out of me. Looking into her face was like looking into the eternal beginning of time down into the end of a pitch dark universe, and then her face changed into the shape of many horrible monstrous features. At least a hundred ugly faces flashed before me within a minute's time. When her face changed back into eternal darkness, a spooky voice came from her face, "Can an angel die? I died, but I came back to life. Everything is not what it seems. Will one willingly become one with a monster? Is he a monster?"

I stood still trembling while fear traced through my veins as she disappeared right before my very eyes. For several seconds, I stood on the sidewalk not knowing what to do. I walked slowly to my car, nervously reached into my pocket for the car keys and put the key in the keyhole to open the car door. My nerves were shocked while driving to Lavon. So many thoughts ran through my mind. The whole episode with the lady dressed in the black cape reminded me so much of the weird dreams I was having. Everything seemed confusing, but I knew there was some connection, and something or someone was trying to warn or tell me something. Trying to figure things out became frustrating and I felt like I should, just as well, stop trying. I wished the spooky scene and mysterious dreams would end and go away before I started thinking I was losing my mind.

By the time I drove to Lavon, my nerves had calmed down and the fear left me as though it was never there. When I pulled up to Lavon, Uncle Zek walked out the salon to meet me. He looked strangely at me and asked, "Debra, are you alright? You look different, like something is troubling you."

In fact, something did bother me, but I didn't feel like trying to explain it all to him because he probably would think I was going nuts, so I lied, "Oh no, Uncle Zek. I'm doing fine. I'm probably a little tired from all the running around this morning." The expression on his face said he didn't believe me, but he didn't push any further. We retrieved the hair supplies out the car trunk and took them inside the salon.

Chapter 6

TYING THE KNOT

On a sunny day at Wayne's parents' house, Wayne and Fernando sat on the back porch under the shade. Fernando took a long drink from a cold bottle of Michelob beer, sighed from the refreshing beer taste and said, "Well, Wayne. The time has come for me to settle down and start a family."

Curiously, Wayne asked, "What are you saying?"

Sitting back in his chair, Fernando answered, "I got engaged, man."

Wayne asked, "To who? That lil' fine honey, Debra?"

Fernando replied, "Yep. I guess she's the one."

Wayne said, "I hope you know what you are about to do. Think about what you have to give up. The three F's, for starters: freedom, friends and females."

With a half cracked smile, Fernando replied, "Yeah...I thought about that, but what you said don't apply to me."

Not understanding Fernando's last statement, Wayne said, "Your decisions are like playing a game of basketball, knowing when to take the best or high percentage shot."

Fernando looked at Wayne with an evil stare and sinister

smile, "Oh, it's a high percentage shot. Deb got everything. She's fine and pretty. On top of that, she got her own business, her own car and house. I think she might be sitting on a nice piece of cash, too."

Wayne replied, "I hear all that, but think about it like this: you're about to take a tough outside shot, but you could make an easy lay-up."

Fernando frowned in confusion. "I don't understand what you mean."

Wayne asked, "Why marry this chick when you can get everything out of her in a regular relationship?"

Fernando answered, "Naw, see…I have to lock her down. Trust me, I got this, man. Besides, I really do care a lot about Debra."

Wayne replied, "Okay…whatever. You care about her. I hope you don't foul out the game, bro."

Fernando said in confidence, "Don't worry. I won't."

Fernando sat telling Wayne the details of his proposal to me and our wedding plans. Wayne listened quietly and suspiciously, wondering exactly what Fernando was really up to. Wayne and Fernando were very close friends, and because they grew up together, Wayne knew by the look on Fernando's face he was up to something concerning the whole marriage situation, but he felt better off not knowing. Wayne assumed Fernando would change his mind because he could tell he wasn't in love with me but only interested in what I had. Wayne said, "All I can tell you is to make sure you know what you're doing because marriage is a big step."

Fernando replied, "Yeah, I thought about it and this is what I want. It's time for my life to take a different turn."

Everything around me seems different, yet I know this place. Beautiful flowers submit along the foot line of tall towering trees. The same lake so often in my previous dreams holds me captive at the edge of a cleft looking down at murky, muddy, raging water. My mind alerts me, "Danger! If you fall, there's no way out of this yuck."

Backing away from the cleft's edge the murky, muddy water waves rise, reaching out for my pain. Stepping backward with heavy leaded feet to avoid being sucked up by big waves, I suddenly turn to the distant voice at my rear. The voice beckons as though he knows me, "Debra...Hey, Debra!" The same man as usual steps forward before me, revealing the owner of the pleading voice. He stands smiling peaceably with towering trees at his back. My vision bypasses his shoulder, uncovering a spooky dark forest behind him.

Fastening my eyes back on the man in front of me, I can now make out some of his facial features. He has a square attractive face attached to a handsome seductive physique. His skin complexion glitters in bronze color. His comeliness infatuates me. He looks to be the perfect man in every way—the man of every woman's dream. Deep down inside, I want to talk with him, but the words won't come out of my mouth. The words resound in my mind, "I know this man and yet I don't know him."

Moments later, he lifts both arms high into the air with something in both hands which I can't make out. He lowers his arms, and in each hand, he holds three dozen mixed roses and carna-

tions. Some are pink, yellow and white. Taking my attention from the flowers and refocusing on his hands, they appear as the hands of dead skeleton bones. I glance back at the flowers, and they had all turned black. He hands me the flowers, but I back away from them. He tries forcing me to take the black flowers, but I continue to refuse. Calmly, he offers again for me to take them. "Don't be afraid. Debra, this is me. Take it. You know me," he said. All I can think to do is run, so I take off running with no destination in mind. He starts running towards me as I turn and run fast as I can, but my legs feel rubbery. My run slows to a trot and then into a slow motion jog. I look down at my body to see what is wrong, and realize I am totally naked with ugly tattoos over my body.

I look back to see if I am still being chased, and what I see literally scares the spirit out my body, causing a clear transparent image of my person to fall out my body and on to the ground beside me. The man chasing me has small worms coming out his fiery flaming face, shaping his beard and mustache. His whole head is made of red hot fire. He holds a big terrifying tornado with both hands, and the fierce spinning force from the tornado pulls at me. Continually, I run, but the pulling force keeps me from putting any distance between us. Gradually, he gains on me and catches me by the shoulders, violently turning me around, pulling my face close to his and kisses me. The heat from his flaming head sends hot chills through the underlining skin over my entire body. His handsomeness, by this time, has totally disappeared.

I try to pull away from him, but he holds me face to face and forces me to look into his horrifying light brown eyes. Wishing for death or to awake, I close my eyes. Slowly, he starts spinning me *around and around, faster and faster. I close my eyes even tighter as I feel myself losing consciousness and full control of all faculties. I feel trapped, caught in a whirling tornado unable to break free.*

After what seems like forever, I open my eyes while lying in bed waiting for my equilibrium to settle. Then I gain a sense of balance and my whereabouts. It feels as though I had spun for an eternity. I lay awake in bed dizzy and dazed. When completely gathering myself, I look over at the clock and it flashes 4 a.m. I blink my eyes and glance at the clock again, and it flashes 7 a.m.

I lay still in the bed for several minutes remembering the terrible face of the man with the flaming head, and the close up look of his light brown eyes sticks in my mind. The only person I thought of with light brown eyes was Fernando. Quickly, I erase any thoughts in my mind that would connect Fernando with the scary man in my dream. The love I have for Fernando is so strong and I can't imagine him being anything remotely close to the man in my dreams, except for the similarity in the eyes. But to me that is neither here or there.

Not sure if I am still dreaming, I get out the bed, walk outside and look around. Lifting my head upwards, I notice not a cloud in the sky. The clean refreshing air revitalizes my soul and spirit at every breath inhaled. I think, "A new day, a new life and a new start—free, free from the stronghold of loneliness and fear, out of the grips of a devil's vortex and out of the storm of hell."

After a few minutes inhaling long hard drags of fresh air, I return inside the house and sit at the end of my bed. I sit quietly listening to the thoughts of my heart which tell me, "One day, all your dreams will make sense."

Eight months after being proposed to by Fernando, I found myself going over wedding plans. Of course, Tasha, Nikki, Carla and my sister, Valerie, would be in the wedding. Tasha would be the maid of honor. Nikki would be in charge of organizing the bachelorette party. Uncle Zek played the father's role of giving me away in marriage.

In the midst of all my excitement while preparing to get married, I couldn't help the feeling of unhappiness because none of my brothers would be at the wedding. Quite a few of my relatives planned to attend. Mom was excited and happy for me, and gave a hand when needed. Everything else seemed perfect, and just like any other woman about to be married, I was equally excited and overjoyed.

For my bachelorette party, Nikki rented two adjoining suites at the Hyatt Hotel located in College Park, Georgia. Nikki asked all the ladies invited not to disclose the location of the bachelorette party so we wouldn't have to worry about jealous women's husbands or boyfriends showing up to break up our fun. Everyone gave Nikki their word not to tell of the party's whereabouts. Nikki especially hid the details of the party from me. All I knew was a big surprise awaited me and I hoped the surprise was in good taste, which I believed it would be.

Some of Fernando's family and friends participated and attended the wedding. Wayne was Fernando's best man, and his friends and relatives were his groom's men. Fernando's friends planned a bachelor party for him, and I made it my business not to ask any questions about their party. I figured Fernando's bachelor party would be on the night before we got married and his friends would provide the party with lots of strippers and alcohol.

I didn't agree with bachelor or bachelorette parties because I felt the parties were a springboard to starting off a marriage on an unfaithful note, especially if one or both persons getting married go all the way by having sex with someone else before the final marriage vows.

I didn't say anything to Fernando about my feelings because I didn't want to spoil or break a long tradition. I knew sex with someone other than with the man I was about to marry was out of the question. I hoped Fernando held to the same standards and integrity.

The night before my wedding, Tasha and I rode together headed to the Hyatt Hotel. We didn't pay attention to the car, which had been following us for several miles. The car was still behind us as we pulled into the hotel's parking lot.

Tasha parked the car and we got out to go into the hotel. We heard behind us a whispering voice calling, "Hey, Debra. Debra. Come here; it's me."

An eerie feeling came over me at the sound of the voice, and Tasha and I turned to see who called out to me. Because of the darkness and distance, I barely noticed the person calling me was Fernando. I said to Tasha, "It's Fernando." Tasha raised an eyebrow in suspicion, giving me a crazy look. I knew she probably thought I told Fernando about the location of the bachelorette party, but I didn't. I whispered to Tasha, "I didn't tell him where the party was. Go on in and let me see what Fernando wants, then I'll be coming in behind you."

Tasha turned to go into the hotel, and I walked towards Fernando as he sat on the hood of his car with his arms folded. Figuring he had been following us, I asked, "Fernando, what are you doing here?"

He smiled, "I couldn't get you out my mind and I wanted to be with you. Besides, I don't like the idea of you being the center of attraction at a bachelorette party."

I replied, "Honey, you have nothing to worry about."

For a moment, I stood puzzled then reasoned within myself, "I don't like the idea of these kinds of parties either. Besides, if Fernando is with me that means he's not at his bachelor party." I asked, "So what are you thinking about doing?"

He answered, "Let's go somewhere and be alone. I know we are not supposed to see each other until tomorrow, but I just had to be with you tonight."

Thinking about my absence from the bachelorette party, I replied, "I have no problem being alone with you tonight, but I have to come up with something to tell the girls inside."

Looking into my eyes, he said, "Come on. Let's go; they'll be alright. They'll figure it out and still have fun."

I thought it was very inconsiderate not telling my friends and relatives I wouldn't be attending a party they prepared especially for me. The feelings inside stirred up a sour emotion in my stomach. Being so bent on pleasing Fernando, I disregarded my better judgment of telling my friends and relatives about the sudden changes. I decided to up and leave with Fernando. I knew some of the ladies at the bachelorette party would be highly upset with me, but I planned later to beg their forgiveness.

Getting inside Fernando's car, I asked, "So, what about your bachelor party? Won't your friends be upset?"

He replied, "It ain't nothing. They'll be alright."

I said, "Honey, we're gonna have a lot of people mad at us."

He replied, "So what? It ain't nothing. They'll be alright."

I said, "Honey, we can't do this…"

With a half grin, he replied, "They'll be okay." We got into Fernando's car and drove off without telling anyone anything.

For the next forty five minutes, we drove slowly around Interstate 285. We talked, laughed and listened to music. We were simply enjoying each other's company. We stopped off at a late night ice cream parlor and wasted two hours talking, holding hands, hugging and kissing each other like two lovebirds. The emotions inside me tumbled because on one hand, I felt such a special romantic mood. But on the other hand, my heart pounded because I didn't show up at my own bachelorette party.

We left the ice cream parlor and drove to my house. Getting out the car, Fernando kissed me. I said, "I guess we won't see each other again until we walk down the aisle tomorrow."

Fernando smiled, "Yeah…I can't wait."

I said, "I love you. See you tomorrow."

He looked into my eyes and replied, "I love you, too, baby. I'll see you later."

Once inside the house, I stood in the bedroom looking down at the flashing light on my answering machine. My heart dropped because I knew there was a string of calls on the machine, and there was no way I could pull myself to call everyone back to explain my absence at the bachelorette party. I had a lot of apologizing to do. When listening to the answering machine to retrieve the messages, the only persons I called back were Valerie, Tasha and Nikki. As soon as I hung up the telephone with them, they were on their way to my house to spend the night to help me get ready the next day for the wedding. They assured me that even though I didn't show up, they still had fun, and the bachelorette party was a success.

Nikki said to me, "At first, the mood at the party was dampened because of the long wait for you to show up. But once we realized Fernando had kidnapped you and wouldn't let you return, we went on with the party. If the girls at the party were upset at anyone, it would be Fernando for coming and taking you." Nikki paused to take a deep breath then continued, "Now let me tell of your surprise. A very fine and handsome male stripper dressed in a nice business suit posed as the hotel's manager coming to bring bad news that the male stripper scheduled for the bachelorette party was unable to make it, due to reasons unbeknown. Being that you were the only one not in on the scheme, all the ladies would pretend to be disappointed by the bad news and start complaining by telling the fake hotel manager he can't let their party be spoiled like that and he had to do something because somebody was going to strip in the room tonight. The fake hotel manager would appear a little frightened and dumfounded as he backed up towards the door to leave while the ladies surround him and start snatching off his specially made tear away business suit. While the fake manager is smothered in between the group of ladies, one lady would switch on the big music box and the fake manager then would emerge from the ladies' midst dancing, wearing only a G-string and necktie. On the other side of the room, five male strippers listened for the music to start then burst into the room stripping and dancing along with all the ladies."

I smiled at their clever plot and was happy to hear everyone still enjoyed themselves without me there. I didn't have to ask whose idea it was because Nikki's hand print laid all over it.

The following day, it all seemed like a dream. I was standing there in a long white wedding dress as the preacher read off our wedding vows from a small piece of paper cleverly concealed in the palm of his hand. I felt nervous and faint as I stared into the eyes of a handsome man who would soon be my husband. I felt jittery and unsettled, knowing practically everyone's eyes and attention focused dead on me. My mind became cluttered, but I concentrated on the cue when to say, "I do." The cue came and I said, "I do," then I breathed a sigh of relief. I was so nervous. It was official. I was finally married and no longer Ms. Debra Williamson, but Mrs. Debra L. Jenkins. This was a special day, and the feelings of joy overwhelmed me. At the wedding reception, I felt like a queen at a celebrity ball sitting high up over the crowd in a chair next to my husband, the king.

After the wedding reception, Fernando and I retreated to the Peachtree Plaza Hotel located in downtown Atlanta. We checked into a presidential suite that Fernando had reserved. The suite was literally decorated and fit for a king and queen. Before entering the suite, Fernando picked me up at the doorway and carried me into the suite and laid me on the bed. The large bed was covered with a French silk bedspread and French satin sheets.

We slowly took our time undressing one another, then we proceeded to consummate our marriage. Fernando kissed all over my body until I felt the heat of passion burning and thundering inside me. We made love many times before, but this time as we began, everything felt so new and different. My body begged for him to enter me. He kept me waiting as his kisses became shorter and rapid, igniting more passion burning inside me. Fernando was now excited, and patience seemed to disappear all of a sudden. He went from slowly caressing and kissing my breast, kissing down to my stomach to suddenly jumping up on top of me and violently thrusting himself inside me. I quickly lost enjoyment because Fernando had his forearm pushed hard against my throat. I kept moving my head side to side trying to avoid being choked to death. I couldn't get the words out my mouth to tell him he was choking me and hurting my neck. He finally took his forearm off my throat, then pushed both my legs all the way up over my head, pressing them into the headboard. I felt victimized as Fernando frantically stroked inside me while holding me hard in some kind of wrestling position. This was not my idea of making love; I felt like I participated in a WWF Wrestling match and I was losing the fight terribly.

Fernando ignored every soft whispering plea I gave, "Honey, take it easy. You're hurting me." My pleas seemed to arouse him even more, so I remained quiet and thought he was just overexcited and caught up in the heat of passion. This rough kind of sex was not my thing, and I hoped this wasn't what he expected when we make love. I had never seen this side of Fernando before. After we were finished making love, Fernando fell asleep. I laid in bed feeling as though I had been raped by a total stranger. I kept the thoughts and feelings to myself because Fernando seemed satisfied, and I figured he would revert back to his normal way of making love to me. For a moment, I didn't know what to think or expect. It grabbed me hard how Fernando appeared to be such a totally different person.

The next morning, I woke to the same type of forceful and physical lovemaking I experienced the night before. After we were finished, we took a shower together. The time drew near for us to check out of the hotel. I said to Fernando while we dressed, "Honey, you are a little rough when we make love—you have to be a little gentler. I'm mainly speaking about the choking."

He looked at me with an expressionless glare. "Try to get used to it. That's how I like it."

I replied, "I don't know if I can handle much more of that."

He said, "Okay. I'll try to ease up a little."

We checked out of the hotel, got in Fernando's car and drove through downtown Atlanta, headed for my house. I sat in the car listening to the music and taking in the sights of people moving to and fro along the sidewalks. Once we got on the freeway, Fernando said, "Debra, I have some of my things in the trunk. I'll wait a few days and go to my apartment so I can move the rest of my things in the house. I'm leaving everything in my apartment except my clothes and other personal items because I turned my lease over to Wayne and Smitty. They already moved in a couple of days ago."

I said, "That's fine. Besides, since we can't go on our honeymoon until later, we need some time alone."

When we walked into the house, Fernando stopped at the door and said, "Debra, I saw how you looked at them guys when we drove through downtown."

His statement caught me by surprise, "What? Fernando, please don't trip. You don't have to be jealous or worry about me 'cause I love you and I don't want to be with any other man but you."

Fernando gave me a strange look, "Okay, I'm warning you."

I nodded my head and walked to the bedroom. Being with someone else was the last thing on my mind.

That little episode with Fernando made me a little suspicious. Briefly, I started questioning my decision about marrying Fernando. His words resounded in my mind, "Okay, I'm warning you." All I could do was hope Fernando didn't change on me and start tripping out now that we are married. However, as always, I kept my thoughts inside and brushed off my thinking in hopes that the little episode would pass and never come up again.

Chapter 7

CHANGING TIDES

Three days after getting married, Tasha and I walked into Glama-Rama, smack in the middle of a make believe forum on male's behavior. The lecture was given by none other than the professional gossip and motor mouth Mrs. Mary. The discussion was so flaring until our entering the salon went almost unnoticed. The atmosphere felt inflamed, but the conversations were not argumentative. The excitement in the air lingered because everyone tried to talk at the same time to get their points across.

All the conversations seemed to flow to and from Mrs. Mary. She propped herself up in a chair like some kind of human relations advisor or guru of love relationships. Curtina Fields, a gorgeous petite beautician in her mid twenties, who looked to be about fourteen years old asked, "Mrs. Mary, why is it that I keep ending up with the same kind of man? No matter what they look like, how they present themselves, or how I pick them, I keep getting the same kind of joker who don't want to work: lazy as hell, and expects for me to give them money."

Silence dominated the salon for a few seconds as everyone waited to hear Mrs. Mary's answer. Mrs. Mary paused as she listened carefully then answered, "Well Curtina, looks like you are doing a whole lot of observing and picking, but you ain't asking no questions."

Curtina asked, "What kind of questions should I be asking?"

Wittedly, Mrs. Mary replied, "For starters, do you have a job? If not, when was the last time you had one? How do you survive without a steady income? Do you live with your momma? If he tells you he ain't had a job in four months, most likely he ain't trying to work. And since we're on the subject, I might as well tell you, Curtina, for the few years I've known you, you have let guy after guy move into your apartment. I blame you and the other women who allow men to move in and lay around the house without a job while you work and take care of them. Women have to stop being so quick to let men move into their homes. A real man will always try to provide a place for his woman to stay. There are a lot of freeloading men looking for women they can leech off of. Some of them are so sorry they can't beat water if they fell out a boat."

Some of the ladies laughed, but Mrs. Mary kept a stern, serious expression as she paused. She looked at Curtina and said, "Raise your standards, child, and that might fix your problem."

By this time, Mrs. Mary captured everyone's attention. She was known for giving such bad advice, but today she seemed to be on point and making some sense. Curtina nodded her head in agreement, letting Mrs. Mary know she took her advice to heart.

One of my long-time, loud and obnoxious clients, Chandra Adams, who we called Ghetto Chandra was in the salon and decided to test Mrs. Mary's expertise. Chandra was only 22 years old, and she exemplified the very epitome of the word, "Hoochie Momma." She had long rust colored fake braids, gold teeth, long decorative finger nails, a million little gold chains around her neck, gold rings on almost every finger, the deep ghetto dialect and wore short-shorts with her butt cheeks hanging out. Chandra asked, "Mrs. Mary, how come every relationship I get in my man end up going to prison for a long time?"

Sarcastically, Mrs. Mary replied, "Chandra, I ain't no psychic, but let me ask you something. Were most of your boyfriends drug dealers?"

Chandra responded hesitantly, "Well...uh...yeah."

Mrs. Mary said, "Chandra, what you are asking is different from what we are talking about. The reason why you keep losing your men to prison is because you like drug dealers, and that's what happens to drug dealers — they go to prison for a long period of time."

Chandra looked a bit confused then casually replied, "Oh..."

Another young attractive client named Taylor Russell said, "Mrs. Mary, I feel like it's some kind of curse on me because no matter what I do to avoid it, certain kind of men are drawn to me like a magnet. I keep ending up with a drug user or alcoholic and before the relationship is over I'm being abused one way or the other. What kind of signs can we look for, and how can we detect this particular type of man?"

Mrs. Mary was on a roll. I saw in her face that she really enjoyed herself and didn't mind the questions being directed at her, "Well, Taylor, I think a lot of women have the same questions and think the same thing about being drawn to the same kind of man, but I still think the problem mainly lies with the woman and her standards and what she is willing to put up with. Just like I told Curtina, ask questions before you get into a relationship because if you ask enough questions, you can get a pretty good idea about what you are about to get into. For instance, when you meet a man just ask, 'Do you get high, or do you like to drink alcohol? What do you think about a man who beats on woman?'"

Interrupting, Tasha surprised me with her input. She wasn't eager to eat up every word Mrs. Mary spoke. Tasha said, "Mrs. Mary, I disagree a little with what you said about getting a pretty good idea of a man by just asking questions. Do you think a man will tell you the truth, when he first meets you, that he is a drug addict, an alcoholic or a woman beater?"

Mrs. Mary wasn't moved by Tasha's questions and responded in confidence, "Yeah, you're right, but listen, honey. If a man won't tell you things about himself, just watch him. I've been on this earth a long time and had my share of dealing with men. When you see a man in a club and he is drinking heavily, most likely he is an alcoholic, and according to studies over the years, most women beaters are alcoholics or drug abusers. They also found out men who are loners, those who keep things bundled up inside and have quick explosive tempers have great potential of being violent."

Mrs. Mary paused as she looked around at all the attentive faces then continued, "See, honey, the problem is still with the women. They are not looking or paying attention to the signs. Some women pick men because they look good, have great bodies and because of their financial status. One of the biggest problems is that men give signs at the beginning of a relationship, but the women don't care or see the signs because the relationship is new and she is excited."

Mrs. Carrie agreed with Mrs. Mary's last comments and even though Mrs. Carrie was not very spiritual, she gave some good spiritual advice to the ladies in the salon, "To add to what Mrs. Mary said, I think the most important thing in finding a good man and the right man for you is to first consult God and wait on the Lord to give you a husband. The problem is most women are picking the wrong man because they don't know how to trust God and wait on God to bless them with a good man."

Taylor said, "I know one thing, I don't have a problem waiting on the Lord to send me a good man now because I'm tired of getting beat up every time I get into a relationship. What scares me is that every time I met a man, he seemed to be loving and kind, then all the ugly hidden things come out once we get used to each other. I'm literally scared to get into a relationship and when I do, if a man hits me one time, the relationship ends there because I will not hang around for a second time."

Mrs. Mary reentered the conversation with more of her advice, "Mrs. Carrie is telling you right, honey. You keep waiting on the Lord. He'll send you somebody. But Taylor, I have to tell you this. From dark skin sister to dark skin sister, I kinda know what you go through. When I used to walk into a setting with a lot of people, a dark skin sister seems to get the least attention. A high yellow or light skin sister always get the best pick of the crop, even if they are ugly and have on fake everything. They still get a man before a dark skin sister will. So what does a dark skin sister do? Normally she settles for whatever she can get. Like I said before, raise your standards and stick to it; you might get better results."

After listening, I had to put my two cents into the conversation to ruffle Mrs. Mary's feathers a bit, "I don't know about that one because different men have different taste."

Mrs. Mary replied, "Debra, you are brown skin and an in between sister, so I don't expect you to understand this. But a dark skin sister will agree with me seven days a week."

I smiled and jokingly said, "Well then, let me shut up."

Tasha jokingly said, "Yeah, Debra, stay out of this." We then smiled at each other for several seconds.

I was surprised at the constructive dialogue between the women and good advice coming from Mrs. Mary and Mrs. Carrie, but I was still a little skeptical of Mrs. Mary because I knew her track record and couldn't help but remember the conversation and position she took when she got into a nasty, heated argument with Ann about her brother abusing his wife.

Ghetto Chandra said, "Mrs. Mary, you should be some kinda counselor or sompin'."

Taking in the compliment, Mrs. Mary smiled, "Yeah and y'all should be paying me sompin'." Everyone laughed at Mrs. Mary's fake ghetto gesture.

After Mom and I went over financial papers and bills for both salons and before leaving Glama-Rama, I talked with Kim to see how she was doing. During the conversation the ladies were having, Kim appeared distant. The whole time she didn't say a word. I knew her problem. She suffered the pain and grief a person goes through while waiting for a mate in prison. She visited Fred at least twice a week, and loneliness started getting the best of her. I didn't want to get involved in her affair with Fred because I knew he still had his girlfriend, Wanda. All I could do was feel sorry for Kim.

Meanwhile, Tasha and I left Glama-Rama to get back to Lavon in time for the clients coming in for their appointments. By the time we arrived at Lavon, Uncle Zek had already opened the salon. No clients had made it in yet, but Uncle Zek said, "Fernando stopped by and I told him you were at Glama-Rama. You missed him by two minutes. He's probably on his way to Glama-Rama."

I asked, "Did he say what he wanted?"

Uncle Zek answered, "No."

I wondered what Fernando wanted so I called Glama-Rama and told Kim if Fernando came by to tell him I was back at Lavon. After one hour, Kim hadn't called back. I called to the house, but Fernando wasn't there to answer the telephone. I didn't expect him to be home because he was supposed to be at work. I also knew he had a little free time in between jobs delivering home and office supplies for Home Depot Supply Store.

Upon finishing my hair appointments for the day, I went home and found Fernando laying across the bed staring up at the ceiling as though something heavy pressed on his mind. Entering the bedroom, I said, "Honey, are you alright? I heard you stopped by the shop looking for me."

At first Fernando didn't move or answer and I stood quiet waiting for a response from him. Fernando slowly turned his head to the side and took his stare from the ceiling and fixed cold, evil eyes on me, "Where the hell you been?"

I answered, "I've been at work. Why?"

He said, "I went by your job right before lunchtime and you wasn't there, and I drove by Glama-Rama and your car wasn't there, so stop lying. Where were you?"

Becoming a little upset because of the interrogation, I said, "Glama-Rama and Lavon are the only two places I've been all day."

Fernando got up from the bed and stepped towards me, "Who are you messing around with?"

Frowning in disbelief I said, "I ain't messing around with no one. You must be going crazy or something."

My comment infuriated him, "What! I'm going crazy!" He drew back his fist and released a punch towards me. Closing my eyes I tensed my face bracing for the incoming blow at my head. Luckily, Fernando's punch stopped within inches of my face as he caught himself and held back his punch. I opened my eyes and breathed a sigh of relief. He pushed me to the side and walked out the bedroom. I stood wondering what in the world all that was about and what I had done.

I walked into the living room where Fernando sat on the couch looking as if he was out of it. I kept my distance and said, "Fernando, apparently we crossed each other when you came looking for me at the salon because Uncle Zek told me you came to Lavon and that I missed you by two minutes and that you probably were on your way to Glama-Rama."

Fernando sat on the couch looking away from me with no

response at all. I said, "If you don't believe me, just call and check and anybody at the salons will tell you where I've been."

Since Fernando totally ignored me, I walked back to the bedroom. I couldn't understand what was going on inside his head. I loved this man and we just got married, but this wasn't what I envisioned as a happy marriage. Fernando's attitude started changing more and more each day. After only one month into our marriage, I found myself swallowing my words and overlooking things to keep peace in our home and to keep from engaging in arguments.

Comic Relief

Thanksgiving of 1991, I went to visit Fred at the Atlanta Federal Penitentiary. He'd been held there since the beginning of 1989. The penitentiary is a dreadful and awful looking place. It reminded me of an ancient library with its carved facing and high peaks. The first time I drove up to the building, it put me in mind of a place where Count Dracula would live. The building looked ghostly and spooky.

This would be my first time visiting Fred since getting married. Going inside the prison placed me on an emotional roller coaster. It broke my heart seeing Fred locked up and not knowing when he'd be coming home. But, he also seemed to put my heart at ease when he walked into the visiting room wearing a big smile, appearing happy. He told me he became a Christian and not to worry about him because he's in God's hand and God's going to work out his situation for the best. I couldn't help but wonder if he told me and the family he was alright just to keep us from worrying so much about him. His demeanor and expressions seemed genuine, so I decided not to question his sincerity.

Every time I visited Fred, we always had fun talking, and it never failed that there would be something unusual to happen in the visiting room before I left. Most of the time when something happened, we were laughing, in tears or sitting silently in deep wondering thoughts. For instance, one Thanksgiving Day, one of the inmates asked his wife to bring one of his favorite foods to him during her visit. Well, of all foods she could bring, she chose chitlings. She smuggled them into the visiting room by sneaking them under her clothes and giving them to her husband. When she put the plastic bag of chitlings into the visiting room microwave, she caused the whole visiting room to stink as the chitlings' smell leaked from the microwave. The chitlings' smell was strong, and the odor smelled as though someone defecated all over the visiting room floor. The visiting room smelled like a raw sewage plant. As black folks would say, "The whole room smelled like pure Do-Do!" Some of the visitors were frowning and looking around to see what caused the awful smell. Other visitors couldn't take the strong odor anymore and ended their visits early.

The visiting room officer walked over to the microwave after investigating where the smell came from. He opened the microwave, held up a see through plastic bag of chitlings and asked, "Will someone please tell me who put this in the microwave?" Everyone in the visiting room glanced over to the inmate and his wife who were responsible to see if they would own up to their bag of chitlings. The responsible couple sat in their seats pretending not to know what was going on.

The visiting room officer turned up his top lip into his nose trying to block the strong aroma. He took the chitlings out the microwave and threw them in the garbage can next to the microwave, then tied the plastic garbage bag, pulled the bag out the trash can and walked the big trash bag out the visiting room as though he carried highly toxic and hazardous biological chemicals.

Another day while visiting Fred, I was shocked when I walked to the vending machines to get something to eat and saw a couple between the vending machines standing up having sex. Pretending not to see them, I simply made a U-turn, went back to my seat and told Fred what was taking place only several feet away from us and that I would get some snacks when they were finished.

The funniest thing I remember is one day I went to visit Fred when the visiting room was very crowded. Different families were forced to sit together, and people sat wherever they could find a seat. I found two seats next to an inmate who visited with his elderly parents. The father appeared to be a little senile. Fred hadn't come into the visiting room yet. I sat so close to the inmate and his parents, and because of the overcrowding, I could hear every word they said. I tried looking around to pretend I wasn't listening to a word they were saying, but I heard everything. The father said, "Son, you know me and ya' momma went to one of those community townhouse meetings to vote and try to get a life sentence for anyone caught selling that crack cocaine stuff."

The inmate asked, "Well, Daddy, how did you vote?"

The father answered, "Me and ya' momma voted yes."

The inmate frowned up at his father's answer and the father asked, "Tell me again, son, what you in prison for?"

The inmate looked disgusted and replied, "Crack cocaine, Daddy, crack! That's what I'm in for."

The father put his hand over his mouth and said, "Oh no. I guess me and your momma messed up."

When Fred came into the visiting room, we spent most of our visit trying to hold our laughs because of all the funny things the inmate's father was saying. Fred and I pretended to be laughing at our own conversation to keep the family from thinking we were laughing at them. We did a good job camouflaging our laughter until the last few minutes of the visit. We couldn't hold our laughter any longer especially when the inmate's father leaned towards him to whisper in his ear. But the tone in which the father spoke was far from a whisper because he talked loud enough for Fred and I to hear every word. The father said, "Son, now I know none of these polices around here trust you, but me and ya' momma—see we trust you, boy. Now come on and walk us to the car."

The inmate looked uneasily at his father and said, "Daddy, this is a high security prison. I can't go to the parking lot."

That was the straw that broke the camel's back. Fred and I laughed so hard until tears ran from our eyes and our sides hurt. It was good for me seeing Fred's ability to still laugh under his condition. Even though we laughed and had high energy conversations during our visits, I always felt depressed the next day after visiting Fred at the prison, knowing I had to leave my brother behind bars and not being able to do anything to get him out. I told Fred about my marriage, and he was happy to see me happy. I tried to get Fernando to come with me to visit Fred, but for some reason, he never wanted to come. Fernando always made an excuse, so after he declined several times, I didn't bother asking him anymore.

Deception Revealed Again

The beginning of January 1992 on a Friday, Fernando called me at Lavon and told me we were going to dinner at his mother's house that night for his sister's birthday. He never asked if I wanted to go or had something else to do. I didn't want to start an argument or say anything to make him feel like I wasn't interested in going to his sister's birthday dinner. I really didn't mind going to the birthday dinner because that meant I didn't have to come home after standing on my feet all day fixing hair and then slave over a stove to get dinner ready. What I really wanted was to go home, take a long hot bath, lie down in bed and rest.

I figured it would be good for Fernando and I to do something together because after getting married, we barely did anything together. When I asked about taking our honeymoon, he acted as if he didn't want to talk about it, so I didn't bring it up again. He actually spent more time over at his old apartment with his friends than with me. I don't know if he really spent all that time at his friends' apartment, but that's what he told me. I didn't want to seem nagging or bothersome, so I went with whatever Fernando said. All I wanted was for our marriage to work. I just wanted to be happy.

Around 7 p.m. that evening at Lavon, the telephone rang again. Uncle Zek answered it, gave me the telephone and said, "It's Tasha; she wants to speak with you."

Tasha had taken the latter half of the day off to take care of some urgent, personal business. Placing the telephone to my ear I said, "Hello, Tasha. What's up?"

Being a beautician, Tasha understood the possibility of me being tied up doing someone's hair or being in the middle of a perm or shampoo, so she asked, "Are you busy? Can you talk?"

I held the telephone trapped between my ear and shoulder while shampooing a client's hair, "I can talk. What's happening?"

Tasha answered, "Debra, you know you are my girl and if something goes down, I have to tell you."

Becoming curious I asked, "Yeah, well what's going on?"

Tasha continued, "Remember the night of your bachelorette party when Fernando came to take you away?"

I replied, "Yeah. How can I forget?"

Tasha said, "Well, later we talked about it and we thought Fernando's bachelor party was the same night as your bache- lorette party. Well, I found out through a friend of mine that Fernando's bachelor party was two nights before the wedding and that he was there the whole night with a house full of naked strippers."

Not knowing what to think as a funny feeling formed inside my stomach I asked, "Tasha, are you sure about this?"

Tasha answered in confidence, "Yes, Debra. I'm sure 'cause I checked it out. What Fernando did was scandalous."

Being stunned for a moment, I became quiet as I held the

telephone to my ear with my shoulder. It was hard to believe Fernando would be so sneaky and conniving. Tasha broke the silence by asking, "Deb, are you alright?"

I answered, "Yeah, I'm okay. Fernando and I are supposed to go to a birthday dinner tonight at his mother's house when I get off work. I'm going to ask him about it."

Tasha said, "Deb, I don't want what I told you to cause any problems. I just had to tell you so you don't keep getting played like a fool."

I replied, "Thanks, Tasha. Everything will be alright. I'm going to ask him and see what he says."

Tasha said, "Okay, I'll talk to you later."

After hanging up the telephone with Tasha, everything she said replayed back in my mind and I thought of how and when to approach Fernando. First, I thought of approaching him the moment I entered the house, but I decided not to say anything until after the birthday dinner when we returned home.

When I came home after work, I didn't say anything to Fernando about what Tasha told me. I took a shower and got ready for the birthday dinner. We went to Fernando's mother's house. Most of his relatives were already there. I acted normal although my insides were turbulent. I didn't want to spoil Fernando's fun with his family. Everyone was having such a good time. They brought gifts for Fernando's sister. Fernando brought a gift on both of our behalf, but didn't tell me he bought the gift until I got in the car and saw the wrapped gift on the car seat. The gift was a beautiful gold necklace.

We came home from the birthday dinner around 11:30 p.m. I

entered the house with some of the birthday dinner leftovers. I walked to the kitchen to put the food in the refrigerator and Fernando walked in the kitchen several seconds behind me. I decided now was the time to ask him about his bachelor party, "Honey, can I ask you something?"

He answered, "Yeah. What?"

I asked, "Did you have a bachelor party two nights before our wedding?"

I looked directly into his face as I waited for the answer. Fernando frowned and his face disfigured from anger as he responded, "What? What are you talking about?!"

I said, "Answer the question. I just want to know."

Fernando ignored me and turned like he was going to walk away then turned back and walked towards me huffing and puffing like a dragon with swollen jaws. He started talking loud, "We had a good time at my mother's house and now you want to mess things up by bringing up some crap! What's the matter? You mad you missed seeing the male strippers at the bachelorette party shaking their butts and slinging private parts all over the place? Is that what this is about?!"

I answered, "No. Don't even try and turn the situation around on me. All I want to know is did you have a bachelor party two nights before our wedding?"

Fernando looked at me with anger and asked, "You want to know?" Just as I opened my mouth to answer, "Yes," he slapped me in the face hard as he could, knocking my head backwards into the refrigerator.

With my back against the refrigerator, the slap and hard force of my head slamming into the refrigerator dazed me, causing me to slide down to the floor. Before hitting the floor, Fernando caught me by the neck with one hand, squeezing tight and choking me as his fingernails dug in my skin.

Fernando held me up from the ground by my throat for several seconds as he looked at the fear buried deep inside my wide open eyes. He saw the life being choked out of me, and just before blacking out, Fernando released his death grip from around my neck and let me fall hard to the floor. My sight and hearing almost completely slipped away as I barely saw Fernando standing several feet away. His loud voice faded back into my hearing. "You satisfied now? This is what you wanted. Are you happy now?"

Sitting on the kitchen floor I backed further away from him as he heralded humiliating insults, planting seeds of fear and low self-esteem into my heart, "Get your sorry, ugly butt up and go to the room before I kill you! And stay there until I tell you to come out! Don't even put it in your stupid mind to try and leave me 'cause I'll hunt your dumb behind down and kill you for sure."

I slowly rose from the floor and walked towards the bedroom and asked, "Fernando, what is wrong with you?"

He looked at me, frowned, tensed his lips and came rushing at me. He pushed me down through the hallway towards the bedroom. He pushed me hard into the walls and shouted, "I said get your ignorant and stupid butt in the room. I don't know what I was thinking by marrying you! Nobody want you 'cause you ain't pretty and you gonna learn I don't play!"

By this time, we were at the front bedroom door and

Fernando shoved me from behind. I stumbled through the bed-room then fell and slid on the floor, crashing into a dresser. He slammed the bedroom door shut and yelled from the other side of the door, "You better not say anything about this to your family or anyone else, or I'll kill them all—starting with your mother first!"

I couldn't believe what happened. The whole experience seemed nothing short of a terrible nightmare. The fear of what Fernando said about killing my family engulfed me. I believed every word he said because I saw the craze and evil in his eyes. I thought, "This can't be real," but the stinging in my face from the slap reminded me it was all so real.

I got up from the floor as my back ached from being slammed into the dresser. I felt the burning sensation from cuts on my neck, which Fernando caused with his fingernails. I walked to the bathroom attached inside the bedroom and looked in the mirror, surveying the nasty scars around my neck. The scars were not bleeding, but the skin was slightly torn, showing the rage in Fernando's handprint.

Tears rolled down my face as I stood looking at myself in the mirror. I thought, "How could Fernando do this to me? How could he be so cruel, low down and conniving?" I didn't know what to do. My world started coming apart. I felt like the gut of my soul was being ripped out of me. I wondered, "How can a man who claimed he loved me so much treat me in such a way?" Then the memories of my childhood came back to me. I thought of the days my siblings and I would fight and the next day, we would be back to loving each other. But this was different and didn't feel the same. This felt so, so wrong.

Fear welled up inside of me so strong until I was afraid to tell anyone what happened to me. I didn't want to tell my girl friends and especially not my mother. My older brother, Carlton, lived somewhere in Mississippi and my two younger brothers were nowhere around. If Fred was home, I would tell him because I knew he would protect me if he knew how he abused me.

Standing in front of the mirror, I wiped tears from my face then turned on the bath water to take a hot bath. I undressed and climbed into the bathtub. I took water in the palm of my hands and lightly splashed it on my face, leaving my face in the cup of my hand as I felt a burning sensation on my neck as water ran down across the nasty fingernail cuts.

After bathing, I got out the tub, dried off, reached in the cabinet for Vaseline to put on my neck, then I prepared for bed. I dimmed the bedroom lights, climbed into bed and pulled the covers over me. I lay awake as the whole episode of Fernando abusing me flashed back before my eyes.

Around 2 a.m., I heard the bedroom door crack as Fernando entered the room. He walked into the bathroom and fumbled around for a few minutes, came back into the bedroom, took off all his clothes and crawled into the bed totally naked. I lay still as he hunched up behind me wanting to make love. He thought I'd fallen asleep and tapped me on the shoulder several times and said, "Debra, Debra. Turn over; I want to make love."

Totally disgusted with him, I rolled over, looked at him and replied, "After what you did to me, I'm not in the mood." Then I turned back over on my side facing away from him.

Fernando rolled on his back, folded his arms and locked his fingers behind his head. He laid in that position for about ten minutes.

Without a drop of sleep in my eyes, I drifted off to another world. I thought Fernando had fallen asleep as he lay still as a rock. Then all of a sudden, I felt the force of his hand chop down in the back of my neck burying my face into the pillow. I moved my head side to side so I could keep from suffocating and said, "You're hurting me!"

Fernando straddled himself over my body, holding me with the force of his elbow piercing down in the center of my back. He took his free hand to reach down and grab the back of my panties. Snatching hard, he ripped them off, causing them to cut and tear the skin in my inner thigh. The pain was excruciating, causing me to scream out, "Aaaahh!"

Fernando placed his hand over my mouth as I tried to break free from him. The more I tried to break free, the stronger and rougher he became. He bent my arm behind my back and sent paralyzing pain through my body. I lay still, too afraid to move because the position and pressure on my arm felt like it would break if I moved another inch.

Fernando penetrated my private. Once inside of me, he humped up and down like he was going crazy. He pushed harder and harder until a horrible sound like a growling creature came from the pit of his stomach. All I could do was lay still because he wouldn't release my arm from behind my back. In a demonic voice, he yelled in my ear, "Move, move your stinking tail around, you whore! Give me some action and excitement!" I just laid there pent to the bed on my stomach in pain and barely able to move. I tried to take a breath and push him off me, but he grabbed a hand full of hair on my head and started humping up and down like he was in a wild rodeo. He groaned with a mixture of laughter as though he got some kind of sadistic thrill and pleasure. Then he climaxed, rolled over and pushed me with his feet away from him to the edge of the bed.

Laying at the edge of the bed felt like I was just beaten and raped by three men. I felt cheap, humiliated, degraded, used and abused. Never in a million years would I believe I'd been raped by my own husband. This became the most violent experience ever perpetrated against me. I felt helpless after thinking about what I should do. For a minute, I thought Fernando was going to kill me. And when he got finished raping me, I thought about killing him, but I had to push the thought out of my head because I didn't want to think like that. I thought about calling the police but said to myself, "It wouldn't do any good." I pictured myself going to the police and saying, "I would like to report a rape."

The police officer would ask, "Do you know who raped you?"

I would then answer, "Yes."

The officer would ask, "Who?"

I would answer, "My husband—my husband raped me."

I became perplexed in trying to figure out how to get out of my marriage. This wasn't marriage, it was a living nightmare! I envisioned a loving husband being a knight in shining armor, always riding up to come aid and save me from danger. Instead, I got the executioner bearing a sharp glittering two edge sword, riding on a black horse, coming to cut me in pieces.

Fifteen minutes after the violent sexual assault, Fernando went into a deep sleep, snoring harder than a man who worked sunup to sundown for two whole days. I lay awake all night long thinking about every dream and vision I had over the last several years. This encounter began to give my dreams and visions meaning and light. Like a bolt of lightening, these words hit me, "Will one become one with a monster?" These were the same words from the lady dressed in the black cape I saw in a vision coming out of Glama-Rama one day.

The next morning Fernando got out the bed, took a shower, dressed for work and left the house without saying one word to me. He saw me laying in bed gazing into the wall, but he acted as if nothing was wrong. I thought, "I hope and pray I haven't married a psychopathic maniac." I hoped Fernando wasn't on some kind of drugs which caused a chemical imbalance, and if so, he would snap out of whatever caused him to act in such a way. This was the man I fell in love with—the man who convinced me he loved me and wanted to spend the rest of his life with me. I had a mixture of emotions shaken together in my heart, leaving me not knowing what to do or which way to turn. I closed my eyes for a moment and pictured myself as a little girl standing outside at night looking up in the sky at the twinkling stars above.

Still unable to sleep that morning, I wanted to just lie in bed. A voice inside me said, "No, you have to get out the house." It had been a long time since I prayed, but I closed my eyes again in shame because I hadn't prayed or talked to God in a long time. I began asking God for help. I didn't know what else to say to

God except, "Lord, please help me. Be with me, I need your help." I lay in bed praying while subtly a spirit of slumber came over me, causing me to fall asleep in the middle of praying until awakened by the ringing telephone on the night stand. I answered, "Hello?"

Tasha was on the other end, "Debra, are you coming in to work? You have two clients here waiting for you."

Jumping out the bed I replied, "Tasha, I'll be there in a little while. Can you cover for me 'til I get there?"

Hearing the tiredness and weariness in my voice, Tasha asked, "Deb, are you alright? You don't sound good. Don't worry; I have things under control here."

I answered, "I'm alright. I'll talk with you when I come in. Let me go so I can get ready. Thanks for calling me."

We hung up the telephone and I headed for the shower. I looked in the mirror at my neck. The redness from the cuts sub-sided, but the fingernail marks were still visible. After taking a shower, I searched through the closet for a turtleneck or sweater to hide the scars on my neck. My entire body ached and felt tired as I dressed for work.

When I walked into Lavon, Tasha and the other beauticians were busy doing shampoos and perms. The air reeked with the smell of hair chemicals. One of my clients was waiting while Tasha shampooed the other client. She looked at me knowing something was wrong. She drew near me and whispered, "Deb, are you sure you're alright? Looks like you had a rough night."

I whispered back, "We'll talk later. Let's take care of these clients first."

Saturdays were always super busy, and sometimes we didn't take lunch breaks. Instead, we ate as we worked. We definitely didn't have the time to talk alone. The only time we'd be engaging in conversation on a Saturday was in an open discussion going on inside the salon with other women. I wanted so bad to talk to Tasha because I knew she was one of the few people I could trust, but I knew it would be hours before we could speak in private.

My spirit tumbled inside me as I listened, not participating in a conversation that already started before I arrived at Lavon. The conversation sounded closely connected to what I just experienced. The women talked about men not understanding how much women go through to satisfy them sexually, the lack of respect and appreciation women sometimes receive in a relationship and how when men want sex—they want it not thinking what women go through during their periods and all the trouble we go through to keep ourselves fresh and clean, or how women worry about telling a man "No" when he is trying to have sex during a yeast infection because he is hard up. And if sex does take place during a yeast infection, they don't consider the painful soreness women suffer. Also, they don't think about the constant checkups at the gynecologist. If a baby is not in the plan, having to worry about getting on birth control and getting the right prescription can be a headache at times—not to mention the cost factor. On top of that, the frequent visits to department stores hunting for Victoria Secret lingerie or other sexy attire to stay appealing to arouse and satisfy men is not ever given a second thought.

The conversation went long and got emotional. The women were really venting and displaying frustration with their men by using harsh words to express themselves. If only they knew what I experienced over the last 24 hours. It seemed as though I stepped into a whole new world which I knew little of; I didn't like it at all.

For the next three hours, I labored like a slave, styling hair until I was interrupted by a delivery guy bearing a bouquet of beautiful and colorful carnations in one hand and a clipboard in the other hand. He came walking through the door, looked at his clipboard and politely asked, "Is there a Mrs. Debra Jenkins here?"

I thought quickly, "Who in the world could be sending me flowers?" I answered the florist, "Yes, I'm Mrs. Debra Jenkins."

Handing me the flowers, he smiled and said, "These are for you, ma'am."

Taking the bouquet of flowers, I said, "Thank you."

I signed the clipboard and opened the small envelope, which I removed from the plastic stem that was stuck in the center of the flowers. I removed the small card inside and read the words, "Baby, I love you. Please forgive me! Love, your husband."

I folded the card, closed my eyes, took a deep breath, opened my eyes as I released my breath and said to the client in front of me, "Can you please excuse me for a minute? I'll be right back."

Everyone looked and said how beautiful the flowers were. One of the ladies asked, "Who are they from?"

I answered, "My husband," then calmly walked to the bathroom at the rear of the salon. I closed the door behind me and slammed the carnations to the floor. I stomped on them in fury, trying to turn them into perfume. I took out my rage on the flowers and had to catch myself before I got too carried away. I did to the flowers what I wanted to do to Fernando. At that very moment, I decided in my heart to fight back if Fernando ever tried and beat me like that again. The thoughts of what I learned in martial arts during my teenage years came back to me. My karate instructor always used to compliment me on the powerful French kick I threw. I didn't remember much about what I learned in karate, but I knew I could still throw a vicious kick.

I didn't want to drift too far away in thought because I had clients waiting on me. So I snapped back to reality, picked up the flowers from the floor, threw them in the toilet and flushed them down the stool. I walked out of the bathroom and finished attending to my clients. Tasha looked at my facial expression and knew it wasn't consistent with a woman happy to get flowers. She knew something was terribly wrong and heavy on my mind.

We worked until 9:30 p.m., and Uncle Zek came to clean the salon before closing. Tasha and I went into the back office to be alone and talk. Tasha asked, "Debra, what's wrong?"

A lump formed in my throat and tears began to stream down my cheeks. Tasha didn't say anything but she hugged me, patted my back and whispered, "Don't worry. I'm here for you, Debbie."

For five minutes, I stood crying on Tasha's shoulder. I needed that hard cry before telling Tasha what happened. I said, "Tasha, what I'm about to tell you, you have to swear not to say a word of it to anyone."

Tasha gave me her word, "My lips are sealed. You can trust me, Debra. I'll never say a word."

I looked at Tasha, then slowly pulled down my turtleneck. When Tasha saw my neck, she closed her eyes and nodded her head side to side and then said, "Oh no, Debra. What happened?"

During the next fifteen minutes, I explained to Tasha the horrific abuse I suffered at the hands of my husband. Tasha suggested I notify the authorities and have Fernando arrested. I explained the danger of exposing him. Tasha stood silent as she searched her mind thinking of some way to help me; she felt what happened was partially her fault because of the news she gave me about Fernando going to his bachelor party. She broke her silence and said, "Wait a minute. He sent you flowers today."

I replied, "Yeah, and on the card it said he loves me and asked me to please forgive him."

Tasha shook her head, "No, Debra. Don't be a fool. He doesn't love you. You have to leave him because if you don't, the abuse won't stop until you're dead."

The fear of him hunting me down like an animal and killing me overwhelmed my soul and I said, "I can't. You don't understand. He's crazy and he'll hunt me down and kill me for trying to leave."

Tasha grabbed both my shoulders and looked me in the eyes, "Listen, Debra. You have to leave. If you stay, he's going to kill you anyway."

Tears rolled down my face again and I said, "I can't leave, Tasha. I'm afraid of what he might do to me and my family. He threatened to kill them, too."

Uncle Zek knocked on the door and said, "It's time to leave."

I quickly wiped the tears from my eyes and then pulled up my turtleneck to cover the scars. Tasha took a deep breath then exhaled, "Alright, Debra. Try to take it easy. We have to find a way to get you out of this mess."

Everyone left the salon and I went home. When I walked inside the house, Fernando sat at the kitchen table rubbing his hand over his hung down head. I walked in front of him and he looked at me with eyes full of tears and asked, "Honey, did you get the flowers?"

I answered, "Yes."

He asked, "Why didn't you bring them home with you?"

I replied, "I left them at the shop——I put them in water. What's wrong?"

Fernando became very apologetic, "Baby, I'm so sorry for what I did to you last night. Please forgive me. I never meant to hurt you like that. I didn't mean those ugly things I said to you. Please forgive me."

Watching his lips tremble and tears stream down his face caused me to feel a little sympathetic to what he said, but the psychological wounds he caused still hurt so much inside. There was no way a few words could erase the pain and heal my freshly open wounds. I asked, "Fernando, help me to understand what it is that made you treat me in such a way."

He softly grabbed my hand and pleaded, "I don't know, I don't know what I was thinking, or what's wrong with me. Please forgive me. I promise this will never happen again."

I stood emotionless, not responding as Fernando begged,

"Baby, forgive me. Please, do you forgive me?"

He looked at me waiting for an answer. I didn't say anything, but I nodded to say, "Yes, I forgive you."

I remained standing as Fernando hugged me around my waist while on one knee. He said, "Thank you, honey. I love you so much. Thanks for forgiving me. I promise it'll never happen again."

He started kissing me all over my face while repeating, "I love you. I love you so much." For some reason, the way he carried on didn't ease the fear inside of me because I had a taste of what he's capable of doing. Although I covered it up, I was still afraid.

For the next few months, Fernando treated me well and acted like the man I thought I married. His violent sexual behavior stopped, and we made love like two normal, sensible married people. We looked to be on the road to a long loving healthy marriage. There was still one problem. Fernando wasn't making much money on his job, and I footed nearly all the bills and loaned him money at times, which he never paid back. It was a good thing I had the real estate venture on the side because that helped keep the financial stress off me. It wasn't a constant income, but when I did have a closing, the commission was good.

I intended not to say anything to Fernando about the problem until I received large credit card statement balances showing he had charged expensive clothing and other things without telling me. When he asked for my credit card, he told me he had to buy a few small things and would repay me when he got his paycheck. When I told him he had to pay those expensive bills, he said, "Debra, I need you to help me out a little. Right now, I'm in the process of finding a better job so I can take care of all my responsibilities."

He tried to put me on a guilt trip by telling me I wasn't acting like a wife, and how our marriage should be totally open and that we should be putting our money together in a joint account. He made me feel bad by saying, "I'm in a bad situation right now, and if the tables were turned, I wouldn't have a problem helping you in any way I could." I wanted very much for our marriage to work, so I went along like a big dummy, merging our accounts and working like a dog so we both could live comfortably. Fernando spent money out the account, knowing he didn't have any money to put back in it. He had no intentions of paying me back. After realizing he wasn't sincere about getting a better job or putting any money back into the account, I decided to open a secret savings account.

August 2, 1992, was my 3-year-old niece Jazmin's birthday. Jazmin was Fred's daughter from his girlfriend, Wanda. Wanda was a beautiful Puerto Rican girl who was five months pregnant when Fred got arrested. Jazmin is an adorable little girl who looks so much like Fred and has very little resemblance to Wanda. Everytime I saw Jazmin, I saw Fred's face.

Jazmin's birthday party was held at Mom's house because her house was big and spacious with a huge swimming pool in the back yard. The kids attending the party ate McDonald's Happy Meals and played in the pool. Uncle Zek made the delicious birthday cake, and he decorated the house with birthday decorations and balloons. Uncle Zek ran around the house and played with the kids after they finished swimming and playing in the pool. He dressed up like a clown and handed out presents to all the children. After the kids opened their gifts, everyone sat down and ate ice cream and cake. Then Uncle Zek rolled out a cart filled with a lot of birthday gifts for Jazmin while the other kids watched her have fun opening the gifts. The kids were having a ball. I looked at Uncle Zek and thought, "What a blessing he is to the family."

Mom and Wanda were having a good time, but I saw on their faces that they missed Fred very much. I talked to Wanda, and she seemed to be holding up pretty good. She really loved Fred and I wondered what Fred was going to do with Wanda and Kim, or how he was going to handle two beautiful women who were deeply in love with him. My wondering came to an end when I went to visit Fred one day and walked in while Kim visited with him. Kim sat before Fred in tears. She was extremely hurt because he told her their relationship had to end, and that it would be best if she didn't come visit anymore because he didn't want to string her along. He said that he wanted to be faithful to Wanda and it wasn't fair for her or Wanda to be in such a relationship. Kim was heartbroken. I felt sorry for her, but it was best for her to go on with her life because Fred contemplated marrying Wanda if his appeal went through and he got released from prison. It was also better for me because Wanda and Kim were my friends, and I felt awkward knowing what went on between them and Fred.

I sat at the table in Mom's house talking to Wanda when (my oldest brother) Carlton's son, Jamal, who was five years old, walked up to me and said, "Auntie Debra, Grandma Gloria said come to her room. She needs to talk with you."

I rubbed his head and replied, "Okay. Tell Grandma I'll be there in one minute." Jamal took off running to deliver the message to Mom.

I walked in Mom's bedroom and she said, "Honey, sit down. I want to tell you something."

I replied, "Yeah, what is it?"

She said, "Well, don't say anything about this, but Uncle Zek is very sick. He has some kind of rare disease and the physicians don't think he'll be living much longer."

My heart dropped. I loved Uncle Zek so much and I couldn't imagine the spark and joyful flare of his presence being taken away. I asked Mom, "What's the name of the disease and how long do they expect him to live?"

Mom answered, "The disease has some long funny name that your Uncle Zek or I can't pronounce. The doctors say they'll be surprised if he's still living by the beginning of next year."

I asked, "How is Uncle Zek handling it?"

Mom answered, "You saw for yourself. He's going on enjoying his life until the time comes. He asked me not to mention anything to the family until the last stages of his life. I'm only saying something to you because Uncle Zek is working at the salons, and soon he won't be able to work anymore. The medication he's on is helping him go on, but in the near future, his whole body will begin to weaken and all his organs will eventually shut down. I want you to pray with me that God will make a miracle happen for Uncle Zek."

Mom and I got down on our knees alongside her bed and prayed for Uncle Zek. After praying, we went back to the kitchen to finish enjoying Jazmin's birthday with her.

When the time came for me to leave, I gave out hugs and kisses and said bye to everyone. When I hugged Uncle Zek, he held me in his arms and whispered in my ear, "Debbie, I love you very much. Your Uncle Zek will always love you."

I always loved the sound and the way he said my name in his Bahamian accent. I didn't want to act in a way to give any sign that I knew of his condition, so I kissed him on the cheek and said, "I love you, too, Uncle Zek." I swallowed hard to keep from crying, and put on the best smile I could muster to hide my emotions.

Mom stood next to me and recognized my forced expressions. She interrupted and asked, "Debra, I'm making some draperies for your Auntie Syblene in Nassau. Can you come back later to help me?"

I answered in hidden emotions, "I don't know yet. If I can, I'll call you."

Mom said, "Okay. You know I'll be right here in the sewing room all day."

Mom had built a large sewing room attached to her house to continue her love for making draperies, and also to make a little money on the side. I walked outside, saddened by the news of Uncle Zek's sickness and got in my car, waved goodbye to everyone and drove home.

Chapter 8

WITHERED FLOWER

Early on a Monday morning in October of 1993, I rushed through the house, getting ready for a physician's appointment. I overslept because during the weekend, I worked long hours and Sunday night I stayed up late watching an excellent movie on the Lifetime Channel. I made sure not to schedule any hair appointments in the morning. Fernando left for work before I got out of the bed. My mind scrambled as I tried to remember all the things to do before the afternoon hair appointments with clients.

Hurrying to get out the house and to the physician's office, I forgot to take some meat out of the freezer to thaw out for dinner that night. Once arriving at the physician's office, the cold October wind brushed against my face, reminding me of the block of frozen meat I forgot to take out of the deep freezer. Hopefully, the physician's appointment wouldn't last long and I would have enough time to return home, take the frozen meat out of the freezer then make it to Lavon in time for the first client.

Just as life would have it, I stayed at the physician's office longer than anticipated and found myself pressed for time to run all the errands before noon. With very little time left before noon, I zoomed into my driveway. Fernando's car was in the driveway and I guessed he must have taken half a day off work. Jumping out the car and trotting to the front door to open it with my keys, a wall of funny smelling odor met me as I entered the house. I heard giggling and laughing coming from the den. Walking towards the den, I saw smoke coming out of the room. Once inside the den, I saw Fernando, Wayne and Smitty laid back on the sofas, high as a kite, giggling and laughing like a bunch of little kids. Beer cans sat on the small tables in front of them and whatever they were smoking still burned in the ashtray. They didn't notice me until I spoke, "Fernando, what's going on in here?"

Fernando looked at me with a serious face and said, "Nothing, we just having a little something to drink."

Fernando's friends tried to hold straight faces, but broke out in laughter. I replied, "And y'all getting high, too. What's that in the ash tray? Marijuana?" Fernando stared at me. I said in a nice way, "Honey, it would be good if you guys don't smoke that stuff in the house."

Fernando said with slurry speech, "Ahh, be cool; it's just a little marijuana."

Smitty looked at me with glassy, blinking eyes, "Yeah, a little marijuana laced with cocaine and embalming fluid. We call it bionic chronic." Smitty then slumped back into the couch and started giggling.

It was obvious they were too high for reasoning. My blood pressure started to rise and I became somewhat angry. The awful smell of death coming from the smoke caused me to turn around and leave out of the room. I didn't have much time left to get to Lavon, so I took the meat out of the deep freezer, dropped it in the kitchen sink and dashed out the door headed for Lavon.

After arriving at Lavon, I worked nonstop until 7:30 p.m. Tasha and I were the only two left to clean the salon after all the hair appointments were done because all the other beauticians already left, and Uncle Zek hadn't been at the salon to clean in several weeks.

I arrived home and received the shock of my life when I stepped through the door. Fernando's angry rage was revealed in the ransacked house. Broken glasses and dishes lay scattered all over the kitchen floor. The furniture was broken and flipped upside down. Holes were punched in the walls from the living room and down the hallway to the back bedrooms. The inside of my house looked like a picture from a war zone. When walking into my bedroom, the sheets and blankets were on the floor, snatched from the bed leaving a bare mattress. Fernando broke the big dresser's mirror and swiped cosmetics and everything off the dresser onto the floor. In the bathroom, the floor was covered with broken perfume glass bottles, and the mirror over the sink was completely shattered. Closing my eyes and nodding my head in disbelief, I said to myself, "Oh no. This can't be happening! It just can't be true."

Opening my eyes and turning to leave out the bathroom, I became startled and frightened to see Fernando standing quietly at the bathroom door. I didn't hear him walk in the bedroom. His eyes were bloodshot red. He looked deranged and crazy as he held a leather belt tight in his fist. He backed away from the bathroom door to let me come out. Too afraid to say anything, I slowly walked out into the bedroom where Fernando stood holding the belt. He approached me, and with a sudden burst of fury, he punched me in the eye and started hitting me with the leather belt while shouting and cursing at me, "You stinking slut! Didn't you know better than to embarrass me in front of my friends, you whore?!" He yelled degrading and derogatory insults as he hit me hard with the leather belt, "You nasty heifer. I'm gonna teach you that I don't play! Your ugly butt blew my high!" The stalking memories of the day Mom's boyfriend, Pete, beat me with a leather belt came back to me.

Being a little dazed from the punch, but still on my feet, I ran around inside the bedroom trying to dodge the swinging leather belt and Fernando's fierce attack on me. Every time he hit me, it felt like the belt ripped a patch of skin from my body. Something told me, "Fight back. Use your French kick," but I couldn't. I couldn't kick or fight back because of my overwhelming fear. After being cornered, all I could do was curl up on the floor to protect my head and face as Fernando whaled away with the leather belt, beating me across the back and legs. The pain felt like fiery electricity shooting through my body.

Fernando beat me until he got tired. I heard him breathing hard as the assault ceased; then he backed away from me. The verbal insults and curse words barely came out of his mouth as his hard breathing chopped up his speech, "Whore, don't mess with me. I'll kill you, tramp." I tilted my head, peeped out one eye and saw Fernando rubbing his head with one hand and stumbling around the bedroom in dizziness.

Still holding the belt in his hand, Fernando looked down at me in a daze. He held the belt, waiting to catch his breath so he could continue his assault on me. I noticed a little red blood slowly running out of his nose. A while back, Fernando mentioned the possibility of having high blood pressure. My guess was that he was right because he definitely had the symptoms of high blood pressure.

Fernando wiped under his nose with his hand and looked at the blood smeared on the back of his hand. He walked to his dresser, opened the drawer and pulled out a small bottle of high blood pressure pills, then walked to the bathroom to get some water to take the pills. I lay on the floor for a moment and began to think, "I'd better get out of the house before he kills me." I uncurled and stood to my feet. Just as I broke out running for the front door, Fernando came out of the bathroom and took off running behind me. Only a few steps behind me as I exited the front door, he leaped forward, pushing me in the back and down to the ground on the lawn. He grabbed my hair then dragged me back into the house.

Crawling on my knees while being dragged back into the house, I saw a few nosy neighbors staring at us. I was sure any minute police sirens would be blaring and policemen would be breaking down the front door to rescue me. It never happened! The neighbors never called the police or came to help. I guess they were just minding their business.

Back in the house, Fernando took me to the bedroom and pushed me onto the bare mattress. I lay on my back while he sat straddled on top of me and repeatedly slapped my face until it got numb. He began tearing off my clothes, but I had no strength to resist his force or fight back. I looked into Fernando's eyes as he ripped off my clothes. I didn't see a husband or the man I married. Instead, I saw a demon man from hell who pledged allegiance and made a pact with the devil to destroy me. Fernando's demeanor became satanic and appeared as though he was a metamorphosis transforming from a man into some kind of demonic animal creature. Then it seemed like a heavy cloud of foul odor covered the bedroom. To this day, I don't know where the strong, awful smell came from. It was a lingering odor I never smelled before. The atmosphere in the room was though an unseen legion of evil spirits ascended from the lowest pits of hell into our bedroom, carrying the ultimate scent of filth and death.

Fernando's eyes were half open, rolling to the back of his head. He began to lick his lips and suck the air as though he tasted the foul odor permeating through the bedroom. He looked like a scene straight out of a horror flick. I was terrified as the foul odor tried to suffocate me and take my breath away.

Fernando tried to have sex with me, but for a moment I resisted. He became extremely violent and forceful. Then, he proceeded to rape me and abuse my body, causing pain while he enjoyed his sick, sadistic thrill. Fernando appeared totally possessed, leaving only the frame of a sane mind. When he finished with his thrill of getting his rocks off, he pushed me aside like a rag doll, then took his feet and slowly pushed me clean off the bed. I hit the floor feeling exposed and unprotected. I crawled under the bed and cried for hours. I felt like dirt. I felt like human trash. My self-confidence and self-worth suffered shock; they were reduced to almost nothing. The fear and psychological effects left me in a devastated emotional state. Over and over I prayed, "Oh God, why me? Why me? What's wrong with me? Am I not a soul worth saving?"

As I lay underneath the bed, I thought back on parts of my childhood. I tried to figure out where I started going wrong and why bad things were happening to me. Even though I recalled the strong spiritual presence inside of me, I also felt some kind of evil, outside forces that were destined to destroy me. I didn't fully understand it, nor could I explain it. Now, a feeling of awareness I gained as a child let me know I was under an unseen attack.

When I was ten years old, I remember going to a swimming pool in my neighborhood, which was owned by a lady we called Mrs. Scott. She charged the kids a quarter each, and we were able to play in the pool unsupervised all day long if we wished. Fred and my friend, Regina, who lived in my neighborhood, Royal Palm Park, went to the pool together. Usually, when we went to swim, I always stayed on the shallow end of the pool because, at the time, I was a little afraid of deep water, and I couldn't swim.

This particular day, I sat on the poolside at the deep end with my feet dangling in the water. Only the bigger kids who were able to swim played on the deep end. I sat splashing water with my feet, and Regina sneaked up behind me and pushed me into the pool, knowing I couldn't swim in deep water. I screamed, "Helllllp!" Fred looked at me and dove in the water to rescue me while I beat water to keep from drowning. Fred swam to me, then he reached out to grab me. I treaded water in full panic, grabbed hold of Fred and wrapped around him tightly like an octopus. He tried to break free and peel me off, but I locked on to him with a death grip. Every time he loosed himself from one grip, I grabbed him somewhere else. We both were going up and down in the pool gasping for air and trying to stay alive while the other kids at the poolside simply watched.

Even though I realized both of us were about to drown, I said to myself, "I can't let go." Fred looked frightened and tried pulling away from me, but I wrapped my arms and legs around his body.

Coming up to the surface for air, I tried to crawl on top of Fred's head. He took a deep breath then relaxed and slowly drifted to the pool's bottom while I held on for dear life. I looked in Fred's eyes and he stared into mine while we sank further down. I held my breath waiting for us to fight back to the top for air, but Fred allowed us to keep dropping; he would not force us back to the top. I thought, "This can't be happening. I know Fred is not giving up on life like this." I couldn't hold my breath any longer and I didn't want to let go of the grip on Fred, but I was a fighter and couldn't drown without trying with everything in me to live.

With no other choice, I let Fred go because I ran out of breath and struggled back to the top to breathe. Back at the top, I treaded water once again trying to keep from drowning while the muscles in my arms and legs burned because of tiredness. Suddenly, I felt Fred grab both my ankles. He lifted me chest level above the water's surface and walked me safely to the pool's edge. I crawled out the pool totally exhausted and laid face down until I caught my breath.

Fred knew if he kept fighting to get me off him, we both would drown. It was smart of him to sink to the bottom letting me run out of air, catch me by the ankles once I headed to the top and walk on the bottom of the pool, carrying me to safety. Thank God we were both alive! Fred and I were totally upset with Regina as she pitifully insisted she was just playing and didn't mean to push me that far into the deep end of the pool.

After reliving that episode in my mind, I flashed back to a time during the mid '70s when the family briefly moved from Fort Lauderdale, Florida to Nassau, Bahamas. Mom had remarried and we lived in a big house in a nice Bahamian community. A large almond tree grew several feet alongside the house, surpassing the roof to about six feet.

One day I followed Fred up the almond tree and he yelled at me, "Debra, get down out the tree! I'll get you some almonds." He looked down from the treetop and yelled again, but I ignored him and continued climbing higher with my sight fixed on a bright yellow almond that was high up in the tree. Determined to reach the almond, I climbed higher from branch to branch. Once I reached the desired limb, getting to the almond was like walking a plank.

Gradually easing out further and further on the flimsy branch, I finally reached out to pick the ripe yellow almond my mouth watered for. Just as I extended my arm to pick the almond, the branch cracked under my feet then broke. All I could do was scream while tumbling down the tree hitting a few branches as I fell. When I hit the ground flat on my back, everything went black and I thought I had died.

Later, I recovered and realized it was a miracle to still be alive. Shortly after, when things didn't work out with Mom's marriage, we moved back to Fort Lauderdale, Florida. Tasha was elated we came back, and when I told her about the incident with me falling out the tree, she jokingly said, "See, that's what you get for leaving me."

Laying curled up under the bed in my drifting frame of mind, it all hit me, "The devil had been trying to kill me for a long time, starting with my early childhood." I thought of other times where my life had been in danger at an early age. It took this horrible abuse to help me try to put everything together. I kept praying and thinking while large portions of my childhood replayed in my mind.

There was no doubt God had been watching over me all the while. Despite my experiences, I survived and was still in good health and in my right mind. God spared my life for a reason, and now it was up to me to figure out my main purpose on earth.

All night I lay under the bed. When morning came, Fernando left for work then I slowly crept from under the bed like a survivor from a nuclear aftermath, crawling out of a cave to assess the surrounding damages. Everything seemed like a bad dream and I waited for it to be over.

I walked to the bathroom bruised, abused and battered. The only thing left to complete the assault Fernando put on me was death. I couldn't get a good look at my whole body and face because the mirror over the sink was shattered. I turned on the water in the tub to take a hot bath. After bathing, I picked up the telephone and called Tasha to ask her to call all my clients and cancel their hair appointments. Tasha kept asking, "Debra, what's wrong? Are you alright?"

I replied, "I'm okay. I'll be alright. Fernando jumped on me again. Please don't say anything about it."

Tasha tried to fish information out of me, but I didn't want to talk. I said, "I'll call you later."

For two or three hours, I cleaned the house and picked up broken things from the floor. It looked like a bomb had been dropped in the center of my house. Fernando had broken a lot of things that were dear to me. He did so much damage in the kitchen until it would be costly to replace everything.

As I swept broken glass from the kitchen floor, the doorbell rang. I wondered who it could be as I ran to the bedroom to wrap something around my head and put on a pair of sunglasses to hide my black eye. Whoever stood at the door knew someone was home because they kept impatiently knocking at the door and ringing the doorbell. I thought, "It has to be Tasha." Opening the front door, Tasha, Carla and Nikki stood on the doorstep. When I saw their faces, I felt so ashamed. Tasha had betrayed my trust. She rounded up the girls and told them everything. She saw the disappointment in my face (because of her) as she looked at me and said, "Debra, please don't be mad at me. I had to tell them. I didn't say anything to anyone else."

The girls walked into the house and couldn't believe their eyes because of the damage and destruction. Nikki said forcefully, "Oh no, Debra. We are taking you out of here. You're coming with us!" I tried to explain and resist, but the girls weren't hearing it. They rushed through the house packing my things.

Carla asked me questions as she threw clothes in a suitcase, "Did you think about taking pictures of yourself and the damage inside the house?"

I answered, "No."

Carla asked, "What about calling the police and getting a police report, or getting your family involved?"

Nervously, I answered, "The police won't do any good and I'm afraid Fernando will try and kill my family if I involve them. He's crazy!"

Nikki said, "You might have to get a restraining order."

Growing more afraid, I asked, "Where are y'all taking me?"

Nikki replied, "To your mother's house."

I pulled back, "No! He'll kill my mother!"

Nikki said, "Don't worry. Trust me. He ain't going to kill nobody; he's a coward for real and is probably softer than hot butter. He's just done a good number on you. He wants to keep you isolated from your family to keep control over you."

What Nikki said made sense, but it wasn't enough to keep me from getting panicky. Carla and Tasha tried to soothe me by assuring me I'd be alright and that someone would always be with me and not let anything happen to me. I went along because the girls were forceful, and they let me know they weren't leaving me there; they would drag me along if they had to. I actually felt kidnapped by my own friends. I submitted, but had to change into decent clothes before leaving the house. When taking off my house robe, the girls put their hands over their mouths and nodded their heads as they saw the nasty belt marks over my entire body.

As we drove to Mom's house, Nikki said, "Debra, you need to call the police to get a report. Take some pictures of your body then go buy a gun. That way, if that sucker puts his hands on you again, fill his butt with bullets. That way the law will be on your side."

I took in everything Nikki said, but I was too afraid to think, and I definitely didn't want to think about murdering anybody. I managed to beg the girls not to tell my mother about Fernando's threats to kill her because it would be too much pressure and stress on her. Once at Mom's house, I told her everything except Fernando's threats to kill her and the family. I couldn't believe all this was happening. When Mom saw my body, tears rolled down her face and she held me lightly in her arms as I cried.

I'm sitting in the middle of a rich, green pasture surrounded by playful baby sheep, which looks like oversized poodles. In front of me stands a big house matching the likeness of the house J.R. Ewing lived in while starring in the hit movie series, Dallas. The house and barn are painted bright white and trimmed in black. There is an all white twenty foot tall picket fence surrounding the entire property. I look through the tall fence into a field of growing wheat, far as the eyes could see.

The pasture where I sit is sectioned off from the house and have the average height picket fence around it. A little sheep walks up to me, and I reach out and rub its head. While gently stroking his head, I look at my hand and notice it is only a bit larger than an infant's hand.

Looking down at myself, I realize I am in the body of a three year old kid, yet I possess the mind of an adult with clear reason-

ing, understanding and comprehension.

The baby sheep in front of me walks away to a larger sheep that stands at a distance as a watchman. The large sheep is the only one of its size, which appears to be the mother of all the baby sheep in the pasture. One by one, all the baby sheep gravitate towards the mother sheep to suck on the nipples hanging from her stomach.

After all the baby sheep are fed, the mother sheep walks over and sits next to me as though I am her owner. I feel comfortable and close to the animal as I sat rubbing the soft wool on her back.

I become distracted because of a kissing sound behind me. The sound is like a dog owner calling his pet. The sound comes from a young man who looks to be in his early 20s, but he has the mind of a toddler. The young man pulls fresh green grass from the ground in a childlike manner, and the baby sheep take turns eating the grass out of his hands.

I watch for several minutes before hearing a squeaking noise coming from the front gate being opened. Two big, hillbilly looking men dressed in blue overalls walk inside the pasture. All the sheep immediately back up to the rear picket fence trembling in fear. The men walk to the rear fence and pick up a baby sheep. I wonder what they are getting ready to do with the little sheep, so I ask them as they are about to leave out the pasture, "Excuse me. What are you getting ready to do with that sheep?"

One of the men looks down at me and says, "Little baby girl, we are getting ready to slaughter this sheep right outside the gate."

I shout, "No, you can't do that right here!"

The man asks, "Would it be better if we took the lamb on the other side of the house so the rest of the sheep can't see it?"

I replied, "Yeah. That would be better than doing it here."

The entire scene changes with me standing on the other side of the pasture behind the barn watching the two men slaughter the baby sheep. Blood from the slaughtered sheep spills all over the two men's overalls and onto the ground. I stand looking, and then a strong feeling of sadness comes over me. I can't understand why the two men are treating the animal so cruelly.

I turn and walk away sad, headed back towards the picket fence. The sheep are inside the fenced pasture playing as before, and the young man sits in the middle of the pasture where I originally sat. I walk to the front gate and open it. Immediately, all the sheep move to the rear of the picket fence. The mother sheep is the only one standing about five feet away from the picket fence while all the other sheep stand behind her in a perfect line with their back end touching the fence.

Puzzled, I say out loud, "Hey, wait a minute! I'm not like those other guys." I try to call the mother sheep to me by motioning my hands, but she stands still looking at me. I focus my attention on the young man and ask, "What's wrong?"

He answers, "Even though she didn't see her baby killed, she knows he's dead."

I reply, "She doesn't know that."

He says, "Yes, she does."

I reply, "Well, I didn't have anything to do with killing her little one."

He says, "She doesn't know that. All she knows is the smell of her baby's blood is on you."

I turn to look at the mother sheep, and the more I stare into her eyes, the guiltier I feel. I hear her mind saying, "Yeah. That

would be better than doing it here." Then, I realize her words are
my words being repeated back to me.

When I awake, my eyes are already open and I am staring up at the white ceiling fixed on two small black dots, realizing I slept with my eyes partially open. A heavy guilty feeling had taken deep root in my heart, which I couldn't seem to shake. I ask myself all throughout the day, "What have I done? Am I to blame?"

Chapter 9

SPIRIT IN THE WIND

I laid in bed waddling in guilt. For the next two days, I stayed in the bedroom. Mom frequently checked on me. Tasha, Nikki and Carla constantly called on the telephone or stopped by the house to make sure I was alright. Uncle Zek's sickness worsened, and he spent very little time outside the confines of his bed. I don't think he even knew I was in the house.

The rest and relaxation I got was much needed. My battered body, although still sore, felt much better. For those few days I prayed, watched television and slept. I hardly ate anything. Mom kept suggesting I eat something, but my appetite was shot, and the fear inside my aching heart kept me from feeling hungry. I knew sooner or later Fernando would call or come over to Mom's house looking for me. Every time someone called the house, I thought it was Fernando. My nerves were unsettled and every time the telephone rang, eerie chills spread over my entire body. When the telephone rang, Mom always answered it; and if the call was for me, she let me know to pick up the phone.

During the third day at Mom's house, the telephone rang while Mom and I sat in my bedroom talking. She picked up the telephone and said, "Hello?" Mom looked at me moving her lips without the sound of words to tell me Fernando was the caller.

On the other end of the receiver Fernando said, "Mrs. Gloria, this is Fernando. Is Debra there?"

Mom answered, "Yes, she's here, but I doubt very much if she wants to talk with you."

He asked, "Can you please ask if she wants to talk?"

Mom replied, "Yeah, but first let me ask you something. Why did you beat on my child like that? I have a good mind to call the police, but Debra begged me not to."

Fernando stuttered and mumbled, "I uh…uh…we uh…we got into a nasty fight and I didn't mean to hurt her."

Mom's expression was as though it hurt to speak with Fernando. "All I can say is I'm very disappointed in you, and what you did to Debra tore up my guts. Hold on, let me see if she wants to talk with you." Mom lowered the telephone to her side and asked, "Honey, do you want to speak with Fernando?"

I didn't say a word, but moved my head, side to side to say, "No."

Mom put the telephone to her ear and said, "I'm sorry, Fernando. She said, 'No.'" Not giving Fernando a chance to respond, Mom hung up the telephone and looked at me as I lowered my head. Mom leaned over and embraced me, then held me in her arms.

Four minutes later, the telephone rang again. Mom picked up the phone receiver and answered, "Hello?" She looked at me and slightly nodded her head up and down to let me know it was Fernando again.

Mom listened while Fernando pleaded with her to persuade me to talk with him, "Please, Mrs. Gloria. Please tell Debra I'm very sorry, and I need to talk with her about something urgent and important."

Mom sat silent as he continued talking. He was in the middle of his words as Mom placed her hand over the phone receiver and said to me, "He says he needs to talk to you about something urgent and important."

I looked at the telephone in Mom's hand, took a deep breath and contemplated whether to take the call or not. I slowly reached for the telephone and placed it to my ear, "Yeah, what do you want, Fernando?"

Right away, he started begging and pleading, "Debra, please. I'm so sorry. I need to talk to you; it's something very important."

I replied, "Go ahead and talk."

He asked, "Can I come get you? I need to tell you face to face."

I wasn't buying it, "No, I don't think so. What do you have to tell me? Just say it on the phone."

Fernando said, "Well, listen. I can't tell you now, but I will tell you later. Right now I have to go. I'm going to call back at exactly twelve o'clock tonight, so make sure you pick up the phone."

Not giving him time to say anything else, I said, "Yeah," then hung up the telephone. I knew Fernando was up to something. I faulted myself for speaking to him in the first place. Now I felt no other choice but to answer the telephone at twelve o'clock when it would ring. It was too soon for me to be communicating with him. I really didn't want to talk with him until much later. From the time we hung up the telephone, all I thought about was the twelve o'clock hour and what was so urgent and important that Fernando had to tell me.

Time seemed to drag by slowly and I lay in bed, hardly able to think straight. It seemed almost unbelievable. I kept telling myself, "All this isn't real. Soon I'll come down from this terrible high, the effects of the drugs will wear off and I'll realize this bad experience I'm going through is not real, but only a bad trip and life's reality for me is nothing close to what I knew."

It was 11:58 p.m., and Fernando sat in a small bar called The Eight Ball, which was located on Bankhead Highway in Fulton County, Georgia. He already drank a few beers before walking to the pay phone next to the bathroom to call Mom's house. Fernando sounded intoxicated on the telephone, "Debra, you need to come home."

I interrupted, "No, I'm not coming back; not right now. What's so important you have to tell me?"

Fernando answered, "Debra, I'm giving you one hour to be standing outside your mother's house with your things so you can come home. If you don't be standing outside, I'm coming in your mother's house with my gun and kill you, your mother and anybody else in the house and then I'm going to kill myself. You know I don't play and I'll do it." Fernando hung up the telephone and I could tell in his voice he was on the verge of doing something crazy.

Once again, fear clouded my mind and gripped hold of my heart, leaving me barely able to think. Placing the phone receiver down quietly, I walked through the house. Mom and Uncle Zek were sound asleep. I returned to my room and silently packed my things. I couldn't put Mom's and Uncle Zek's life in danger, so after packing my belongings, I sat quietly in my room until close to the time to be standing outside.

Fernando drove in his car on the way to Mom's house. The time drew near for me to reenter Fernando's hellish world and presence. Falling alongside the bed on my knees, I prayed for God's divine protection. I decided not to wake Mom and tell her about my leaving, but instead, I would call her the next morning and tell her I returned home to try and work things out in my marriage. Even though I wanted so bad to tell Mom the truth, I couldn't because I didn't want to scare her.

At 12:50 a.m., I sat on the front doorsteps outside Mom's house waiting for Fernando. He pulled into the driveway at exactly one o'clock. He swung open the front and back passenger door. I put my things in the back seat and climbed in the front seat. Fernando looked at me but didn't say anything. I glanced down at the chrome plated handgun as Fernando put the car in reverse and backed out the driveway. I didn't say a word while Fernando drove home. I didn't want to say anything because I didn't know what went through his head. I feared I may trigger something in his head and face a brutal assault when we got home.

Fernando broke the silence, "Debra, I didn't want to do this, but you make me crazy sometimes. Part of how I act is your fault. We were doing fine in our relationship until you embarrassed me in front of my friends. I mean…I lost it. You are the one who provoked me."

I listened while Fernando talked. He was explosive and unpredictable, so the best thing for me to do was hold my peace. He continued, "You keep pushing my buttons making me do stupid things. Have you ever thought about that? Maybe you are a part of why I act this way. Just think about it and you'll see where you are wrong and make just as many mistakes as I do. I want things to work between us. You see, everybody make mistakes. We are all entitled to mistakes. Sometimes you make me doubt whether you love me…"

Refusing to break my silence, I listened to the words Fernando spoke until they started affecting me. I sat quietly, convinced some other force or entity spoke through Fernando, craftily forming and structuring his sentences to make me feel guilty for what happened to me and our relationship. I felt confused and foolish. Fernando really was doing a number on me. I sat in the car looking out the window as I thought, "Can I be causing my own abuse and deterioration of our relationship? And have I really been provoking him?" I searched my mind to see what I did to warrant such violent attacks and brutal assaults perpetrated against me, but came up with none. I thought, "Why am I putting my brains through this torture? All I ever did was try to make our marriage work. Maybe I'm not the perfect wife, but I hadn't done anything for Fernando to assault and beat me half to death."

Once we got home, Fernando began to beg for forgiveness. He cried and begged me to give him another chance. I was too afraid to say no because he probably would beat me again. Even if I didn't mean it I told him I forgave him and was willing to give him another chance, because to me it was better than being beaten and having my family threatened to be killed.

That night before we went to bed, Fernando opened up and poured out his soul to me. I listened to him with caution, thinking maybe this was another one of his plots or schemes to manipulate me. He went on and on about being abused as a child, and how he watched his father beat his mother. He stated that was part of the reason why he resorted to violence most of the time. I wanted to tell him, "Don't leave out the drugs and alcohol," but I kept those thoughts to myself. For some reason, he couldn't see my feelings and hurts, or recognize the fact that he took his anger out on me because of something done to him in his past by someone else. I thought, "Maybe violence is all he knows and that his parents didn't teach him not to be violent. Maybe he needed to go back home to live with his parents and learn all over again how to grow up, be a real man and learn how to treat and communicate with a woman." He definitely was out of control and his only reaction to conflict ended in violence.

I knew if Fernando heard my thoughts, he probably would want to kill me for sure. Living with him caused me to literally pay attention to every action or reaction to not provoke him to awaken or stir up that mean monster inside of him. I found myself walking light and talking low in my own house.

Calling Mom the next morning and telling her I returned home to try and make my marriage work didn't set well with her. The tone in her voice let me know of her disappointment and that she was against me going back to Fernando. She didn't try to influence me to leave him. She just didn't know how bad I wanted to leave him, but it just wasn't that easy for me to up and leave.

I took everyone of Fernando's threats seriously, and if only Mom knew the whole story, she would understand. I felt like a sacrifice for my family by staying with Fernando, and they weren't even aware of it.

After eight days, my scars and bruises healed pretty good, and I returned to work at Lavon. For the next two weeks, Fernando took me out to dinner after work and sent flowers, balloons and chocolate candy to my job. It was routine for me to take the gifts straight to the bathroom whenever the delivery guy brought them to Lavon. I stumped the flowers on the floor, threw them in the toilet, smashed the boxes of chocolate and threw them in the trash can and burst the balloons. I knew the people in the salon wondered what I did with all the gifts. For some strange reason, Fernando thought flowers and candy was all it took to make everything alright in a relationship, and when he sent the gifts, he had done his part in fixing the situation.

Fernando got to the point where he wanted to control every part of my life. He treated me like a child, having me to ask for everything with childlike humility. He became exceedingly jealous and started accusing me of messing around with guys, which was not true. I gave him all my love and faithfulness and held our marriage sacred. Somewhere in the back of Fernando's demented mind, he thought I had a secret relationship going on with a guy, and that, eventually, he would catch us. It probably was the drugs and alcohol playing tricks on his mind.

After two months when I returned home, the cycle of violence started again and he made up any reason to beat me. The beatings weren't as severe as before; mostly, he punched me in the face or head, pushed me down to the ground and called me nasty names. I think the conversation he had with Mom may be the reason why he didn't go all out in violence against me. At times when I acted as if I wasn't up to having sex, he violently raped me or forced me into sexual intercourse. My body still got bruised, but not as bad as before. Since the day I returned home, sex with Fernando was always unpleasant.

I became exhausted and depressed from the psychological, physical and emotional abuse. I was also depressed from being trapped in the house, isolated from everyone. Fernando constantly called me terrible names until I started feeling ugly, unattractive, stupid and not wanted by anybody. I couldn't understand what was happening to me. Normally, I'm in control, but now my thinking was off. Many times I thought about when I attended college and used to tell Carla how beautiful and attractive she was. I knew she had a negative self-image of herself. Everything in me said I was right about my thoughts of Carla being verbally abused at an early age. I figured Carla had experienced some kind of verbal abuse by someone close to her which affected her psychologically and destroyed her self-confidence. At first, I couldn't understand why Carla thought she wasn't beautiful, but after what Fernando put me through, I understood the possibilities of Carla's way of thinking. The spirit of low self-esteem and negative self-image tried to totally overtake and perpetuate itself against me. This was another battle waged inside of me. Constantly, I fought against the mounting negativity of myself. Though the negative feelings persisted for a time, I refused to give in to them. My whole life became a fight to survive and it was a must to maintain my sanity.

One night while at home, Mom called and I answered the telephone. She asked, "Honey, is Fernando home?"

Curiously, I answered, "Yes."

Mom said, "Tell him to come to the phone. I need to speak with him."

I placed the telephone down and walked to the back room and said to Fernando, "Pick up the phone. My mother wants to speak with you." I wondered why Mom wanted to talk with him.

Fernando's forehead wrinkled, making a funny facial expression as he picked up the phone receiver, "Hello, Mrs. Gloria. This is Fernando."

Mom said, "Fernando, this Sunday our family is coming together to discuss a serious family matter concerning Uncle Zek's sickness, and it's important for Debra to be here. I'm calling asking you to make sure she is at my house by six o'clock in the evening if you both don't have anything planned. Fernando, for whatever reason, Debra hasn't been spending time with the family. I'm counting on you to make sure she is here because it's very important."

Fernando replied, "No problem, Mrs. Gloria. I'll make sure she's there."

Mom said, "Thank you very much," and then hung up the telephone.

Skepticism covered Fernando's face as he turned and looked at me, asking, "Debra, what have you been telling your mother? Did you tell her I keep you isolated or something?"

I answered, "No. It's obvious; you don't let me go anywhere.

I guess Mom feels you are the one keeping me from coming over to her house like I used to."

Fernando replied as though he was given direct orders from the President, "Well, on Sunday at six o'clock you are going to your Mom's house. She said your family is having a special gathering to talk about something serious dealing with your Uncle Zek's sickness."

Mom called around to gather all her children at her house on Sunday evening. Uncle Zek insisted all Mom's children be there with the exception of Fred. Uncle Zek looked very weak, but he managed to cook a fantastic Bahamian dinner with little help from Mom. He wanted to do most of the cooking because this was a special time for him. Despite Uncle Zek's sickness, he pulled himself together to enjoy dinner with everyone. The food tasted absolutely delicious!

It was evident death walked near and upon him. He looked really weak and tired, but he still mustered up enough strength to tell a few jokes and make everyone laugh. After we finished eating, Uncle Zek reached for his walking cane and slowly walked around the dinner table headed for the front door. In a weak, fatigued voice and rich Bahamian accent, he said, "Everybody, follow me. I have somethin' to show you."

Everyone walked out of the house following him to dead center of the front yard, which was surrounded by beautiful flowers, short hedges and a nicely landscaped structure. Uncle Zek stood for a moment looking high into the sky as though he looked at something great and fixed in its definition.

We all looked up at the beautiful baby blue sky tattered with

slow drifting silver lined white streaky clouds. Uncle Zek pointed his index finger up towards heaven and said, "Everybody
look. Look way beyond those clouds. Can't you see that beautiful place? There is where I'm going. I'll be high up there beyond
the deep blue yonder." Some of Mom's children looked at each
other strangely, silently implying Uncle Zek may be going senile.
They knew Uncle Zek was a little sick, but they didn't know he
was soon to die. Mom and I knew automatically what he meant.
Uncle Zek took it upon himself to explain, making clear exactly
what he meant, "Never...never once do I want any of you to
worry or feel sorry for me. You see, your Uncle Zek is about to
die and pass over to the other side. I don't want you to feel sad
when you think of me. I want you to feel joy—-joy because I'll
be in a wonderful place."

Uncle Zek never once took his eyes off the sky when he
spoke. When he finally lowered his head, he looked at Mom and
I. Tears were streaming down our faces. Uncle Zek reached over
to wipe tears from both our faces and said, "Oh no, no. Don't cry
for me; be happy. Uncle Zek is going to be alright. I lived a good
and joyful life. Don't be sorry for me. I'm ready...ready to go on.
Promise me you won't cry anymore." He held my face in his
hands and kissed my tears and said, "Promise me you won't cry."

With tears still rolling down my face, I nodded my head up
and down.

Uncle Zek hugged and kissed everyone on the forehead while
we stood on the front lawn, then slowly turned around with his
cane and walked back into the house. Everyone slowly followed
him back into the house. Two days after everyone returned home,

Mom called around to inform us Uncle Zek died. He had lain down in bed to take an afternoon nap and never woke up.

I found comfort knowing he didn't suffer terribly through his sickness before he died. He simply laid down in peace, closed his eyes and slipped over into eternity. Somehow, I think Uncle Zek knows how much we all love and miss him. Though we miss his presence, our hearts are settled because we believe he is in a better place.

Chapter 10

TURNS OF LIFE

For months, I felt like a slave and prisoner in my own home. Though never doing time in prison, I knew firsthand what it felt like to be imprisoned. I lived under the custody of an evil and wicked prison warden: my husband! I felt so trapped—like a hostage with no way out. My situation was terrible and nothing in my house seemed beautiful anymore. Besides, Fernando had destroyed most of my things and burned a lot of my clothes. He wanted me to dress like an old-fashioned woman with long dresses and everything covered up. His jealousy became sickening rather than flattering.

By this time in my life, many things had changed about my inner feelings. Although Fernando couldn't destroy the value of my heart, he did manage to dry up the constant free flow of feelings that once ran like a river of life, permeating through me. Now I felt empty, barren and desolate inside. My love turned to fear then slowly into disgust. I knew if things didn't change eventually, I would despise the very sight of my husband. Sometimes when I looked at him, it was as if I looked at the devil himself. Every ounce of love and respect I had for Fernando slipped away, and our pledge of love disappeared at every encounter of abuse, dishonesty and unfaithfulness.

I spent my life going to work and coming home. Fernando wanted to account for every minute of my life. He began taking my car keys after I came home from work. He went through my purse and took my address book. If I needed to go somewhere, he dropped me off and picked me up. I asked him, "Why do you take my car keys every time I get off work?"

Feignly, he answered, "We don't spend enough time together, so I feel we can work on getting a closer relationship if I drop you off and pick you up when you need to go somewhere. This way I can work on building a stronger love for you."

I listened to his explanation, and we both knew he blew a bunch of smoke. I knew exactly what he was doing. He wanted to know my every move, but the moment I asked about where he was going, he wanted to beat me up.

I came home from work one Saturday evening and noticed Fernando's clothes laid out on the bed. Figuring he would be going out that night, I got upset because three days prior I asked Fernando if I could go to a comedy club on the weekend with Tasha and Nikki, but he said, "No. I need you to stay home with me." It was obvious he didn't plan on spending any time with me.

I made up my mind to confront him about where he was going and face the peril of abuse for asking, "Fernando, how come you can go out when you want and I can't? I asked to go out one night with my friends and you said no, but you go out when you want."

Fernando turned and looked at me with a frown and began to

approach me. I stood still, bracing myself for a blow to the head or face. He walked within inches of my face, took his index finger pushing it into my forehead, causing me to stumble backwards several steps and yelled, "You want to go to a stupid comedy club with Nikki—go ahead!" I stood surprised with a suspicious look on my face. I started to speak, figuring he was up to something, but decided to hold my peace and not say a word. I turned and walked out of the bedroom. I knew he was messing around with some woman, but I really didn't care. I hoped one day he would come home and say he was leaving me for the other woman so I could be free once again.

I called Tasha and Nikki and told them to include me in their plans that night because I was going to the comedy club with them. I needed to get out the house before I went crazy behind those walls. A good laugh might be the kind of therapy I needed to help pick myself up because my spirit had been down so long.

Within two hours from the time I came home from work that day, Fernando had taken a shower, gotten dressed and left out of the house without saying goodbye or where he was going. I took a shower, put on a pair of jeans and a nice sweater then drove to Tasha's condo. We then drove to Nikki's house, picked her up and traveled to Pinky's Comedy Club, located outside Atlanta in a city called Smyrna. We paid at the door and walked into the club. The first comedian had just come to the stage when we walked into take our seats. For some reason, he immediately zeroed in on me. He started picking on me as if his whole comedy skit was prepared and centered around me. I thought, "Is something wrong with me that I don't know about, but everyone else can see? Why do I have to be the target?"

The comedian stood holding a microphone up to his mouth, "How y'all doing tonight?" Whistling, cheers and applauds came forth from the audience as the comedian pointed at me. He waited for the noise to die down, "Hey you…the fine lady in the blue jeans and sweater." Nikki and Tasha knew I was getting ready to be picked on for laughs because they were about to let loose their laughter before the comedian got to his punch line. He continued while looking straight at me, "You know…you remind me of a fine, sophisticated project girl I used to date named Lisa. She tried to be classy and smart, but she was dumb as a pile of bricks. I mean she was so dumb she barely had enough common sense to fit inside a raindrop. To make matters worse, she had a gay brother who liked to play the piano. The first time I went to Lisa's house to visit, her gay brother sat at the piano dressed in a colorful costume with glittering beads and sequins covering it. He played the piano looking like a black Liberace. I spoke to him as I entered their house, 'What's up, Niggerace?' He sucked his teeth, rolled his eyes and started singing at me, 'There's a fool who walked in my house.' He kept playing the piano and making up words to the songs to insult me."

The audience erupted in laughter. The comedian continued, "Then Lisa came out from the bedroom dressed in an expensive outfit looking like a project version of Diana Ross. I took her to a nice, exclusive restaurant. We had a cozy candlelight table smack in the middle of the restaurant. You won't believe this…she put her Fendo purse (a knock-off Fendi designer pocketbook) on the table and just as we were about to give each other the romantic stare, I noticed a big cockroach crawling out her purse. I looked and said quietly, 'Uh...you have a little insect coming out your purse.' With a quick swipe of her hand, she knocked the cockroach into the air sending it sailing to a lady's back who sat at a table next to ours. I watched as the cockroach crawled up into the white lady's long blonde hair.

Lisa sat up in her chair giving me a sexy look, acting like nothing happened. Just as I got ready to say something about the second cockroach crawling on the table from out the side of her purse, the waitress walked up to take our order. The waitress saw the cockroach on our table and started apologizing. The waitress thought the cockroach came from somewhere inside the restaurant. She didn't know Mrs. High Class infested the restaurant with a bunch of big muscle bound cockroaches."

By this time, some of the people in the audience were literally rolling on the floor in laughter, holding their hurting sides. The comedian was in his groove and had the audience captured, but I wasn't feeling him. He looked at me and said, "Baby, you ain't got no big cockroaches in your purse do ya'?"

With a slight smile, I slowly moved my head side to side to answer, "No," while the audience looked at me and cracked up in laughter.

Thank God, the comedian took his focus off me because he started laughing at his own joke. He continued his skit, "Hey y'all, let me tell you how dumb this girl was. When the waitress asked to take our orders, I told the waitress, "I'll try the filet mignon with the special chef's mustard sauce." Lisa looked in the menu like she couldn't make up her mind what to order so I asked, 'Why don't you try the filet mignon also?' She shrugged her shoulders, gave me her best sophisticated pose and said, 'Naw, that's alright. I don't like fish that much.' She was so dumb that if her I.Q. dropped another point, she would probably go into a coma.

Nikki and Tasha really thought that punch line was hilarious. They were laughing so hard, tears rolled down their cheeks. It took me several seconds to pick up on the punch line because I had almost forgotten filet mignon was beef and not fish. Little did they know I felt just as dumb as Lisa. Being in an abusive marriage with Fernando and taking all the ill-treatment hit me like a ton of bricks. I thought, "How can I be so dumb and stupid staying in an abusive relationship?" The thought didn't last long because I immediately remembered why I was still in the marriage, and it had nothing to do with love anymore. The core of fear apprehended me and I recoiled back into fear's grip.

The comedian really got off on his own jokes. He laughed just as hard as the audience, then regained himself and said, "Before I leave the stage, the moral to this story—you is what you is, and not what you ain't, so be who you is and not what you ain't."

I sat at the table watching comedian after comedian come to the stage telling jokes. I wasn't in the laughing mood, but pretended to smile at times when Tasha and Nikki thought something was funny and looked at me for a response. My body sat there with Tasha and Nikki, but mostly my mind drifted somewhere far, far away. Actually my mind was thinking, "Why did God make humans out of flesh? Instead of making us out of meat,

God could have made humans out of steel or some other super strong material. That way, when being kicked in the ribs and stomach, or punched in the face, the blows wouldn't hurt so much." No matter what I did, these were the kind of thoughts that constantly haunted me. Sometimes, it felt like I was going out of my mind.

Tasha and Nikki knew my marriage situation and wanted so much for me to have some fun. I may not have had fun listening to the comedians, but I did enjoy Tasha's and Nikki's company and being out with them. I savored the moment because there was no telling when I'd get the chance to go out with them again. Even though Tasha and I worked together almost everyday, it wasn't the same as going out together.

Tasha and Nikki were having a ball of fun, and their happiness satisfied me. They were my girls and I loved them. Being with them made me feel good and gave me a sense of being. I hated when the night came to an end because I knew we'd have to depart. I dreaded having to go back to my own house and say goodbye to my friends. Inside of me wanted to be rescued, crying out to them to help me, but I could never get it out or get the message across to them. I felt stuck inside myself!

I dropped Tasha and Nikki off to their places and returned home about 1:30 a.m., but Fernando hadn't made it in yet. He crept in the house around 4:30 a.m. I felt him ease in the bed. I lay still, pretending not to notice his presence. Twenty minutes later, I heard him snoring lightly. I wondered, "Is he treating his other lover like he treats me?" My world seemed completely torn apart and I had to do something to change it; but what?

177

As weeks and months passed, Fernando's attitude towards me grew colder and colder. The hate in his heart towards me seemed worse than what he would have for an enemy when all I did was try to better his life.

One time during this period, I encouraged Fernando to attend a business seminar in Atlanta with me. I wanted to get out of the house and do something. He agreed to go. I signed up for the both of us and paid the fees. Before the seminar started on our first day, I went to the bathroom then returned and walked up the hallway. Fernando and a female stood talking with each other. When I approached them, he stopped talking to the female then introduced us. I said hello to the young lady and proceeded to walk to the seminar.

Fernando got angry at me, but I didn't know it. At lunch break, he grabbed the skin on my arm, pinching and piercing it with his fingernails and pulled me across the street as we walked to the car. While he pulled me, his fingernails penetrated deeper into my skin until my arm began bleeding. We left the seminar to go home, and he beat me up for not getting jealous because he talked to another woman. I had to think fast to stop the assault so I said, "I trust you 'cause you're my husband." It worked and he backed off, but that was the end of our seminar.

I guess Fernando wanted me to be jealous and experience his all-too-familiar feelings of jealousy and rage. His jealousy had really worsened and he snapped at any time. Mostly when he drank a beer, he made up things to accuse me of messing around on him, then he abused me sexually and locked me in the bedroom like a dog for hours at a time. He became so jealous that when a man complimented me one day while walking in the mall by saying to Fernando, "You have a beautiful wife," he freaked out and beat me up once we got home.

He asked, "What did you do to make the man say that?"

I was in a no win situation. It didn't matter whether we stayed home or went out; he always found a reason to abuse me. I suffered many days of abuse because of this mystery man Fernando accused me of messing around with.

I became only a tool and convenience to him. I denied myself to put Fernando first in everything, and both our lives were all about pleasing him with no regards for my feelings. My feelings for him died almost completely after the second major assault on me, and since then, I felt trapped in the marriage. Every sensible part of me warned, "Get out of this relationship because it is all wrong."

I received no love at home and my heart ached just to be loved. Fernando never said, "I love you," or, "How was your day?" He didn't show any interest in things concerning me. In fact, he never remembered our anniversary. I didn't remind him, but let our anniversary day go by like any regular day. I stopped looking for those kinds of things from him, yet I needed to hear I was still beautiful and desirable. The emotional well of love inside me dried up when it came to Fernando, and I found myself slipping into depression. It is a horrible feeling not being loved, cared for or respected by the very man who is supposed to be your husband. I felt numb inside. I envisioned a happy marriage, us doing the simple things lovers do, like tickling each other under the arms and feet while in bed or giving each other a kiss just because. I never imagined this—not in a million years. The great gulf of emptiness in me thirsted for the need to be filled and loved.

Though Fernando slowed from physically beating me, the mental abuse increased and seemed as bad as the physical abuse. I wished for the abuse to stop, but it didn't. One day, I rushed home from showing a client a piece of commercial real estate to make dinner for Fernando so he wouldn't have to wait to eat once he got home from work. I made spaghetti, cooked mixed vegetables, baked garlic bread and made delicious fruit punch Kool-Aid. Fernando sat at the table while I brought his food. When I finished serving him, I placed my food on the table. I sat down and Fernando asked, "Debra, where's the salad?

I had totally forgotten to make the salad. I said, "I'm sorry; I forgot."

Right away Fernando got mad, "You forgot! What you mean you forgot!?"

I saw the crazed look in his eyes warning me trouble was on the way, and I fearfully replied, "It's no problem. I can make salad in one minute."

Fernando looked at me with cold, hateful eyes, "It is a problem. You know to make salad with spaghetti. I tell you what, I'll make sure you won't forget the next time because you are going to eat every bit of food on this table or wear it!"

Right away, I lost my appetite, but started to slowly eat my food. Halfway through my plate, I couldn't eat anymore. I placed my fork down and sat back in the chair. Fernando stared at me then said, "What are you doing? Keep eating until you finish."

Lowering my head, I replied, "I can't eat anymore."

He burst out in anger, "Do you think I'm playing with you?!"

I didn't answer or move a muscle. He picked up his plate of spaghetti and threw it in my face. He threw every piece of food on the table at me. After covering me with hot spaghetti, he took the Kool-Aid and poured it on top of my head. I sat calm, soaked in Kool-Aid and covered in spaghetti. As Fernando walked away from the table, he shouted, "Now clean up this mess, you stupid idiot! I'm going out to get something to eat!"

Going off on me for forgetting to make salad was his excuse to get out of the house and take his mistress out to dinner.

While cleaning up the mess Fernando made, I felt a mixture of bad emotions running and tumbling through me. I pondered in my mind, "I'd be better off if I confess my sins to God and ask for forgiveness to secure a place in heaven, then lay down to sleep and pass on to glory to the place Uncle Zek pointed at in the sky when we all stood in Mom's front yard."

I had gotten to the point of being sick and tried of feeling afraid and abused. I said to myself, "If I die, I die." I accepted the fact that death was just another part of life. Something had to change because I couldn't go on living this way. I thought about what Nikki said the day she, Tasha and Carla came to kidnap me from home to take me over to Mom's house when Fernando assaulted me with a leather belt. Nikki said, "Fernando isn't going to kill anybody because he is a coward who managed to do a good number on you."

I noticed a bit of reverence Fernando had for Mom. In a sense, he kind of cowered down to her when she spoke with him—not in a negative way, but in a sense of respect. I had to take my chances that Fernando was only bluffing about killing my family, and leave from under his abuse and humiliation.

Early the next morning as Fernando walked out of the house for work, I started packing my things in two suitcases. I decided to go back to Mom's house and plan my next moves from there. I dashed through the bedroom collecting everything I needed. I called Mom on the telephone and told her I was coming over to her house. I didn't tell her the reason because I planned to once I arrived there.

After hanging up the telephone, I hurried through the front door, opened my car door and threw both suitcases in the back seat, and drove to Mom's house. Arriving at Mom's, I received the shock of my life. Mom opened the front door and I walked in with both suitcases in both hands. Placing both suitcases on the living room floor, I sat on the couch and said, "Mom, I need to stay here for a while because I'm tired of living with Fernando. We've been having problems.

Mom looked at me concerned. "Debra, listen, honey. You have to make up your mind what you want to do. You can't keep jumping in and out of situations. I suggest you go back home to Fernando until you are sure and confident you can't take it anymore. That way, when you decide to leave again it will be forever."

At that moment, I couldn't explain the horrible feelings rushing through me. I felt like a bombshell dropped on my head, causing my whole body to explode. I wasn't just hurt; I was devastated. If I couldn't go home to Momma in times like this, where else could I go?

Quietly, I politely picked up both suitcases, walked out of the house, got in my car and proceeded driving home. So much turmoil went on inside me while driving. I felt mad, resentful and angry towards Mom all at the same time. To me, this was the height of rejection, and I questioned Mom's love for me. I guess you can call this tough love or some kind of reverse psychology Mom used to help me make up my mind about leaving Fernando.

Mom didn't understand the fact that going back to that slave dungeon of mine could cause me my life. After a few days of rationalizing, I realized Mom loved me, and in a sense, I knew she was right and that when leaving Fernando, my mind had to be made up to leave for good. The initial shock of Mom's words caught me off guard because they were unexpected.

I thought about years back when my sister, Valerie, got married and went to stay at Mom's house a few times because of minor spousal abuse from her husband. Mom used the psychology of sending Valerie back home; it worked, so I guess Mom thought the same would probably work on me, but I didn't think so because the situation was different.

I couldn't really blame Mom or expect her to fully understand my plight when I hid things from her without telling her the whole story. Mom probably thought I would come to her house for a few days then sneak away in the middle of the night like I did before, returning back to Fernando.

A short time after my failed escape to Mom's house, the physical abuse grew more intense at each incident, and Fernando sensed my fear to leave him so he had his way with me. I was just an old rag doll he could throw around. I found myself hiding scars and black eyes more and more. Fernando used to be very apologetic after he abused me, but all that had stopped. He had absolutely no regard for my feelings anymore.

Every dream of a good life I had seemed shattered with no chance of being mended. I never imagined that life could be so cruel and unkind. "Lord, have mercy on me," I said. I cried enough tears to fill the Nile River. To make things worse, my finances became strained because of costly medical bills that were due as a result of abuse and time off work. This was the result of a badly bruised face. If I was able to hide my scars and bruises, I went to work. I stopped my real estate business for two reasons. Firstly, because of bruises on my face and secondly because Fernando followed me around and showed up out of nowhere when I would be showing a male client a house. Fernando's sudden appearance and suspicious demeanor frightened some of my potential homebuyers.

I went into a deeper spiral of depression, and the feeling of loneliness grew stronger. Though there were many faces around, I still felt alone in a big world with no one to really turn to but God. I was afraid to turn to Tasha, Nikki and Carla because their resolve was too drastic and radical—not understanding the true sudden dangers of lives at stake. They would probably come and swoop me up like eagles and fly me away.

At this point in my life, all I did was cry and pray to God night after night to help get me out of this mess. Nothing seemed to change, and I doubted if God heard my prayers. Many nights I lay in bed unable to sleep, but I had to stay strong to survive and escape the perils of depression and anxiety.

On a sunny Saturday afternoon, I walked into Glama-Rama, surprised again to see women talking about the exact subject I faced at home. Although a lot of gossiping goes on in a beauty salon, there's so much to learn about life during the many ongoing conversations and dialogues. Sometimes, it felt as though I was the only one facing new experiences in life that no one else experienced. The salon gossiping sessions let me know what I was going through was far from new and that I wasn't the only one facing certain dilemmas.

I decided to listen and hold my comments while the women spoke because I didn't want a bunch of nosy, gossiping women prying into my personal business. It's bad enough some of them knew about my abuse at home.

Mrs. Carrie often showed compassion and sympathy towards what I went through at home. She pulled me aside whenever I came into Glama-Rama and asked, "How are you doing, baby? Is Fernando, the sicko, behaving himself? I know it's hard to leave sometimes, but get out of that situation soon as possible." No doubt, her concern was genuine, and just knowing someone cared made all the difference in the world to me.

Gail Horton, a beautiful full figured lady in her early 30s, poured out her heart in front of all those women as I sat in an empty salon chair listening. Gail said, "I'm just disgusted with my relationship at home. I'm tired of being taken for granted and ignored. I mean, my husband forgets our anniversary. He doesn't remember my birthday, and if my daughter reminds him, he still doesn't do anything special for me—no gifts, birthday cards…nothing!"

Mrs. Carrie asked, "Well, Gail, honey. Did you bring this to his attention?"

Gail answered, "Yeah, a couple of times, but now I don't bother. Our relationship is so dead it feels like I'm just going through the motions, waiting for it to end. The fire burned out a long time ago and I can't even explain why I'm still in this stupid relationship."

A young lady named Faye Myers jumped into the conversation, "My situation is the same. There are no flames or fire in my relationship, either. I've been living with my man for two years, and he refuses to marry me. In my home, there's no love, peace or happiness. When we go places together and get around family and friends, I become invisible. He carries on and talks to people as though I'm not there. He never says anything to compliment me. I told him the biggest problem I had is being totally ignored and neglected by him, but it did no good—in one ear and out the next."

Vanessa Coles, an attractive newlywed in her mid 20s sat under the hair dryer. She said, "Since I got married, it seems all my husband wants to do is come home from work, sit in his Lazy-boy reclining chair and watch television."

Vanessa looked at Faye and said, "Faye, girl, I feel ya' 'cause I get no attention from him until we get in bed. Sometimes it feels like I'm a roommate sharing an apartment. I even entertained the thought of moving to a separate room. The only good thing I can say is he don't run the streets, he brings his pay check straight home after work, and only takes about thirty dollars out for the week."

Mrs. Carrie replied, "Baby, you're in a better position than a whole lot of women. If he don't run the streets and brings his money straight home to you, be thankful because to many women, he is considered a good man."

Everyone made comments and little gestures in agreement, then Mrs. Carrie continued, "Trust me. I know what most of you ladies are going through. In my first marriage, I stayed home taking care of kids. At first, being a housewife appeared to be a great idea, but in a sense, my husband used that to control and keep me dependent on him for everything. I had no income to take care of myself or buy anything I wanted. Our relationship took a bad turn, and I felt stuck with no way out of the marriage. When I finally broke up with my first husband, I walked out the door with only the clothes on my back, but I gained a sense of being and freedom. Afterward, I picked up and went on with my life."

Sitting in the salon chair listening, I realized I had heard many of those kinds of conversations while working in the hair salon before getting married, but the words never stuck with me or held much meaning. Now every word rung loud and clear, and I hung on to every word spoken. I thought about the state of many women facing similar circumstances, but at the time no one's situation seemed as important or serious as mine. The women talked of being ignored and neglected, but I faced brutal physical, mental and sexual agony. I faced the same problems as theirs and more. Maybe some of them were experiencing physical abuse, but no one mentioned it. I could understand them taking that position because neither did I want to share my story of abuse with them. Deep down inside, I wanted to share my plight with someone, but my better judgment warned me to keep my mouth shut in the salon if I didn't want my personal life story in the streets or all over town.

For another twenty minutes, I sat in Glama-Rama listening and learning from the women's conversations, which jumped from subject to subject. Everything the women talked about seemed relevant to my situations.

The things said at Glama-Rama soaked down into the sponge of my spirit, and tears rolled down my face as I drove back to Lavon. I thought of a three-way telephone conversation I had with Nikki and Carla several days before. They were talking about their marriages in an attempt to get me to open up and talk to them about my marriage. Their plot only depressed me more because Carla spoke about putting everything before herself and not doing anything she wanted to do, yet not complain too much because it was a small price to pay because they had a pretty good marriage.

Nikki seemed to have the perfect marriage and couldn't ask for a better husband, although she tried to complain a little and only ended up realizing how blessed she was. I think when talking about their spouses, they got caught in the passion of their own affairs and forgot about my horrible situation. Don't get me wrong, I was happy for them and didn't want to hurt their feelings by saying, "Girls! Please! I don't want to hear about your wonderful marriages right now." Walls of negative energy bombarded me as I thought of the terrible state of my marriage. I kept my words inside and dealt with the emotional devastation I faced on a daily basis.

Embedded Rage

Fernando, Wayne, and Smitty walked through South DeKalb Mall in Decatur, Georgia, around 7 p.m. Fernando watched while his friends ran around like kids trying to pick up on girls. After an hour of walking through the mall and unsuccessful attempts of getting telephone numbers, they decided to go play basketball at the Wesley Chapel gym, which stayed open until 10 p.m.

While Fernando drove, they engaged in a conversation. Wayne said, "Fernando, man, I have to find a good woman like you got. Since you got married, you don't want for anything, and you always keep some of that good supersonic weed. I remember your days of struggling. Boy, you came up on a good one."

Fernando smiled slightly and replied, "Wayne, your problem is you're looking for Mrs. Right. Stop trying to find Mrs. Right—-it ain't gonna happen. You have to get a woman you are attracted to then work on molding and shaping her into what you want her to be. You got to make her Mrs. Right."

Smitty interrupted and asked Fernando, "Oh yeah, and how do you make a woman Mrs. Right?"

Fernando answered, "I'm going to let you guys in on a secret you probably already know, but haven't given much thought. Have you ever noticed the more you mistreat a woman, the more she falls in love and is drawn to you, and the more you fall in love with her and treat her good, the more she dogs you out or runs over you?"

Wayne said, "What are you saying? Mistreat a woman and you stand a better chance of shaping her into Mrs. Right?"

Fernando replied, "What I'm saying is, if you are in love with her, don't let her know how much. And when she steps out of line or acts up, don't be afraid to tear her butt up. After touching them hips up a few times, she'll be like a puppet on a string. She'll submit and do whatever you say. It's just like training a dog, but if you fall in love and be all lovey dovey, she'll have you like a puppet on a string."

Smitty looked at Fernando to see if he was serious about the words he spoke. Realizing Fernando's seriousness, Smitty replied, "I remember the last time we got high at your house, and it looked like Debra called the shots and had you like a puppet on a string because we ain't got high at your house since."

Wayne and Smitty burst out in laughter. Fernando didn't find Smitty's comment funny; he frowned with a stone cold face as he responded angrily, "Oh yeah, you think so? Trust me, Debra will never pull a stunt like that again."

Smitty asked, "What did you do, beat her up or something?"

Fernando paused then answered as anger continued building inside, "Yeah, something like that! It makes me mad thinking about how she tried to play me!"

Smitty and Wayne looked at each other with raised eyebrows and suspicion. Wayne said, "Fernando, you have to learn how to chill and stop getting mad so easily."

Fernando and his friends drove to the gym. Once inside, they saw that the basketball courts were full, and several groups of ballplayers waited in the bleachers for their turn on the court. Fernando realized it would be at least 30 minutes before they would get to play. Smitty said, as he climbed in the bleachers, "Well, guys, I guess we can park it here until our turn comes up."

With a nasty attitude, Fernando snarled, "I'm not waiting here all night behind these guys to play. Let's go!"

Smitty begged, "Come on, Fernando. It's not going to be long. We came here to play ball and have fun!"

Fernando responded aggressively, "Come on, let's go! I'm headed to the car!"

Wayne and Smitty climbed out of the bleachers and followed Fernando while the guys in the bleachers gave Fernando ugly looks. Walking out the gym door Wayne asked, "What's up with you, Fernando? What's wrong?"

Fernando answered, "Nothing. You guys can stay here if you want, but I'm going home."

Smitty replied sarcastically, "Okay, we'll stay if you leave us your car."

Fernando said with a blank face, "Yeah, right…"

Getting in the car, Smitty and Wayne shook their heads in disgust. Fernando remained silent, but he was clearly angry as he drove Smitty and Wayne back to their apartment. Knowing Fernando was mad, Smitty and Wayne sat quietly also. When they reached the apartment, Wayne and Smitty got out of the car without saying goodbye and slammed the car doors. Fernando looked at them, gritted his teeth and drove off, burning rubber.

Chapter 11

GETTING LIFE BACK

I had been home a little over an hour after finishing my last hair appointment at Lavon. The telephone rang as I walked out of the bedroom to take some dirty clothes to the laundry room. I dropped the clothes basket on the floor in front of the door and hurried back into the bedroom to answer the telephone. It was Tasha on the line. She called to remind me not to forget to order more hair relaxer or get some from Glama-Rama because we were running out at Lavon.

Fernando's keys rattled in the front door and I heard him walk into the house. Tasha and I continued talking. My back faced the bedroom door so I couldn't see Fernando when he walked up behind me. He startled me by standing inches from my ear and whispered, "Who are you talking to?"

I turned nervously and looked at him before answering, "This is Tasha."

I saw the deranged look in his eyes and knew trouble was on the way. I spoke in the phone receiver, "Tasha, I have to go. I'll call you back later."

Tasha heard the strange sound of my voice and asked,

"Debra, is everything okay?"

I answered, "Yeah, Fernando is standing here."

Tasha said, "Okay, call me back."

Fernando stared at me for a few seconds and said, "What is the clothes basket doing in the doorway?"

I answered, "I was taking them to the washroom when the telephone rang."

Fernando asked, "Are you sure that was Tasha on the phone? Why did you have to say I was standing here?" Fernando walked right up in my face. I didn't try to explain, so I kept my mouth shut. Fernando said, "Heifer, you better not be having some guy calling this house while I'm not home." I didn't respond because I saw the look in his eyes and knew he wanted a reason to physically abuse me.

I tried to side step Fernando to walk around him, but he grabbed and pushed me on the bed, "Where are you going? You're not going to walk away from me like that!!"

Crawling out of the bed towards the door I said, "I have to go and wash these dirty clothes."

Fernando walked towards me and said, "Naw, you're trying to disrespect me." He pushed me into the wall then reached out his hand to go for my throat. Being fed up and not wanting to take the abuse anymore, a voice spoke inside me, "Fight back!" My reflex and instinct activated as I used a karate technique to block his hand going for my throat. My reactions caught him off guard as I blocked his hand, grabbed his wrist, pulling him towards me and threw a straight hard French kick in his upper stomach, knocking all the wind out of him. Fernando grabbed his stomach, bent over and fell to the floor gasping for air. I stood over him not knowing what to do next. The thought of killing him ran across my mind, but I didn't entertain the idea long because I knew I wasn't a murderer.

Fernando moaned, groaned and rolled on the floor like he was dying trying to catch his breath. I turned to go in the bedroom for my extra set of car keys so I could leave before Fernando regained strength. Heading for the front door with my keys and purse in hand, I looked down at Fernando moaning in a weak voice, "Debra, please help me. Don't leave me or I'll die. You hurt me bad."

I stopped in my tracks and had compassion as I looked at Fernando lying curled up on the floor in pain. He stopped moving, but continued moaning and groaning. I paused for a moment and slowly walked in front of him. When Fernando realized my presence in front of him, he leaped up from the floor with the quickness of a cat. I jumped and backed away from him into a karate stance. He rushed me as he hollered and threw punches, "You tramp! You're going to get it!" I backed up throwing kicks and wild punches to hold him off, but he came at me with the anger and fury of ten men. He was too big and overpowering until I could no longer stand against his strength. Fernando grabbed my throat with one hand, and with the other hand he punched me hard in the face. The blow was so vicious it felt like my whole face caved in. Everything went blank as I fell to the floor. I came back to from a hard kick in the ribs, which lifted me several inches from the floor. I could hear him calling me horrible names as he picked me up from the floor by my hair. Holding me against the wall to get a clear shot at my stomach, he hit me hard as he could, dropping me to the floor again. I thought I was going to die as he commenced kicking me in the ribs, head, face, chest, legs and buttocks until he got tired.

Fernando walked to the kitchen to get a glass of water, leaving me on the floor bleeding and in pain. Chills ran through my body as I heard Fernando breathing hard over me and the clicking sound of his teeth knocking against the glass while he drank the water. After finishing the water and violently smashing the glass against the wall, he hollered, "I'm going to teach you a lesson once and for all!" I knew what that meant, and tears flowed down my bruised face as Fernando started kicking me again. I thought, "He's trying to kill me and I'm too weak to help myself." Everything started going black, then shortly after, I regained consciousness by another painful kick to the body. I almost went into shock as I lay on the floor in excruciating pain.

Fernando walked to the back room and returned with his chrome plated handgun. He placed the hard cold barrel to my head as he stood huffing and puffing to catch his breath. With fuzzy and blurry eyes, I barely could see him standing in a trance looking down at me contemplating whether to pull the trigger or not. The fear and terror was so intense in me that I felt hot flashes of chills like a zillion little needle heads tingling under my skin. Lying on the carpet, I prayed to God inside my heart, "Oh God, please don't let me die. Please help me."

Moments later, Fernando put the handgun in his waistline, picked up my car keys from the floor and grabbed both my ankles. My head bumped the corners of furniture as he dragged my limp body over the floor towards the front door. Once outside and lying on the driveway pavement, he opened the car door then stuffed my battered body into the front passenger side floorboard.

I could hardly breathe and my entire body ached. Every time I inhaled air, the throbbing pain in my ribs intensified. I didn't know what Fernando planned to do, but I did know he was up to no good. I began to pray harder, asking God to save me and not let Fernando kill me. Again, I hoped the nosy neighbors heard or saw something that would prompt them to call the police, but no one ever did.

Fear dominated my entire body as I wondered what Fernando thought about doing to me. He didn't say a single word as he drove around the city of Atlanta looking for a safe place to finish me off and dump my body. Ninety minutes passed and Fernando continued driving around in a daze. After two hours and not being able to find a satisfying place to kill me and dump my body, he decided to take me to DeKalb Medical Hospital. Before arriving at the hospital he said, "Debra! Listen, I'm going to take you to the hospital. When the physicians ask you what happened, you better say you fell down the stairs. If you don't, I'll make sure I kill you next time. You're supposed to be dead right now anyway. I don't know why I haven't killed you yet." I lay on the floorboard listening; I was hardly able to move a muscle. He shouted down at me, "Do you hear me?"

I hurt so bad, the words barely came out my mouth, "Yes…yes." He repeated over and over again how he would kill my family, starting with my mother, if I implicated him.

Fernando drove into the emergency parking lot, parked the

car, got out and walked to the passenger's side and opened the door. He looked down at me and said, "If you don't cooperate with me, people in your family are going to die." Fernando had beaten me so bad I couldn't walk. He picked me up in his arms and carried me as though he was a loving and caring husband. He trotted toward the emergency room while I bounced up and down in his arms. When the nurses saw my battered body, they put me on a stretcher and tried to lay me down straight, but it was too painful for me to stretch out because the muscles in my ribs and stomach felt knotted up, so I stayed curled in the fetal position while they rushed me to the emergency room.

The nurse asked Fernando what happened. He lied, "I don't know. I think she fell down the stairs or something. I came home and found her on the floor curled up at the bottom of the stairs." I thought as I listened to Fernando lie, "We don't have stairs in the house."

He held my hand as medical staff wheeled me into a small room inside the emergency room. Once inside the little room, Fernando stepped outside the door to get out of the way. The nurses asked questions as they attended me. Fernando paced back and forth in front of the door, looking into the small room to see or hear what was happening or being said.

A physician came into the small room, and right away, he recognized the signs of domestic abuse. He took a quick look over my body then turned and looked back to Fernando pacing outside the doorway. The physician placed his clipboard on the bed, walked to Fernando and asked, "Excuse me, sir. Is that your wife?"

Fernando replied, "Yes."

The physician said, "Well, we're going to admit her in the hospital and run a series of tests to find out what's wrong. So you said you found her like this when you came home, huh?"

Fernando answered with the expression of concern, "Yeah, that's right."

The physician said, "Okay, we can handle it from here. I'll ask that you please leave the emergency area, but you're more than welcome to wait in the lobby as long as you wish, or leave information at the counter so we can contact you as soon as we find out what's wrong."

Fernando took a last glance at me then disappeared. The physician walked back into the small room and asked, "What happened, dear?"

Barely able to talk and body full of pain, I lied, "I fell down the stairs."

Compassionately, the physician paused, "Listen, Mrs. Jenkins. I know what happened, and if your husband is responsible, all the police need is a report from you and they'll lock him up." I didn't say anything in response as tears flowed.

The next morning, I woke up in a regular hospital room after the medication wore off. Opening my eyes, I saw Mom seated at the bedside while she held and rubbed my hand. She had been there for hours praying while I slept. I looked at the tears in Mom's eyes, and the first thing she said was, "Baby, I'm so sorry."

My body ached, but I mustered up a slight smile and said, "It's okay, Mommie." She reached and lightly rubbed my head and face as tears welled in her eyes. I felt her motherly love and care with every touch.

I wondered how Mom knew so fast of my admittance to the hospital, then I remembered the phone call from Tasha. The night before, she sensed in my voice that something wasn't right. When she tried getting back in touch with me and couldn't, she went into action to find out my whereabouts.

Mom said, "Don't worry, baby. You're going to be alright. I spoke with Dr. Miller, and he told me you have a light concussion, a few bruised and fractured ribs and a little internal bleeding, but you will be fine. Just get some rest and don't worry about anything. The family and I are right here for you."

A nurse came into the room to give me more medication, and before it took effect Mom said, "Debbie, tomorrow the police will be here to talk with you and get a report."

I mumbled in agony, "No, Mommie. If Fernando finds out I told on him, he will try to kill you and the family."

Mom interrupted while patting my hand lightly, "Don't worry, baby. I know what's going on. I know about Fernando's threats. Carlton, Oliver and Kenny will be at the house so you don't have to worry about Fernando trying to kill anyone." Mom left so I could get some rest, and shortly after, I gave way to the medication's effect and fell asleep.

The next day around 11 a.m., I awoke to a room filled with family and friends. My brothers were steaming mad and wanted to kill Fernando. I heard Oliver in the background saying, "I'm going to kill that sucker." Mom took Oliver outside the room and talked to him alone, begging him not to kill Fernando.

Tasha and Carla didn't say much, but looked at me shaking their heads in disdain with tense lips. When Nikki saw my badly bruised face, she was astounded, "That nigger is dead wrong! His day is coming. He's going to get his!"

Nikki left the room because she couldn't stand seeing me in such bad condition. She was smoking mad. Mom did her best to keep the atmosphere from flaring, but there were a lot of emotions stirred up in my room.

Seeing everyone gathered around my bed in support and deep concern really made me feel loved and cared for. Even though everyone was angry because of what happened, in a way, my pain and suffering was comforted by the show of love coming from them. For a long time, I felt unloved by those closest to me, but now I felt loved and protected by everyone's presence. My heart had longed for this kind of love.

The nurse came in the room to feed me around 11:45 a.m., but I didn't eat much. At noon, two police officers entered my room with a pad ready to take a report from me. Everyone left the room and waited outside except Mom, Nikki and Tasha. They practically begged and encouraged me to tell the policemen what happened. The time came for me to make an intelligent and conscientious decision. I told the officers of my fears concerning Fernando coming to the hospital to finish me off then carry out his threats against my family. One officer said, "Don't worry. We'll have security posted outside the door until we get him off the street, and if he makes bond, we'll have security return."

Nikki made sure she mentioned to the officers about the time Fernando physically abused me with a leather belt and trashed my house. After the officers retained all the information needed, a warrant was issued for Fernando's arrest and the police picked him up the same day. The next day Fernando's family paid his bond and he got released right back on the street. It puzzled me how a human being could treat another person so cold, cruel and ruthless. What Fernando did to me is a crime, and he needed to be locked up in a jail cell somewhere.

Later the same day after everyone left, Dr. Miller came into my room and checked on me to see how I was doing. He greeted me with kindness and said, "You did the right thing talking to the police, Mrs. Jenkins." Then he paused and said, "I have something to tell you and I don't know how you're going to take it. Just know I am here to help in any way I can." Right away, I braced myself for bad news because of Dr. Miller's facial expression and demeanor. He continued, "Mrs. Jenkins, when we ran tests on you, we discovered that you are pregnant. Although you received tremendous blows to the stomach, because of the early stages of conception, your pregnancy wasn't terminated. However, I feel your pregnancy is nothing short of a miracle."

Pain streaked through my body because my bruised ribs expanded when I took a deep breath, closed my eyes and exhaled. I thought to myself, "If it ain't one thing, it's another." Dr. Miller stood at the bedside waiting for my response, but I said nothing. I paused while contemplating having an abortion and hoped for a miscarriage so I wouldn't have to carry the burden of guilt and shame of aborting a child. Even though I forced the thoughts out of my head, I still felt guilt and shame for considering an abortion.

Dr. Miller left the room as I lay in bed thinking and it hit me, "What's there to think about? It's a miracle I'm still pregnant. What's growing inside my stomach is precious and a part of me. I can't destroy that!"

My life seemed a mess and nothing made sense. And to get through this ordeal I knew I had to involve God in my every thought and in everything I did. Lying in bed, I realized the Lord heard my prayers and came to my aid to save me because I was still alive. I remembered Fernando's eyes the night he assaulted me, and there's no doubt in my mind his intentions were to kill me.

I took birth control pills prior to getting pregnant, but at times, being unstable and distraught because of abuse, I forgot to take the pill some days. By missing days on the birth control pill, my cycle was disrupted, opening a window to increase the chances of pregnancy. The last thing I wanted was to be pregnant by Fernando. A child from him only complicated things and tied him deeper into my life. Being pregnant wasn't number one on my list of problems. The biggest problem was getting Fernando out my life.

After three weeks and finally being able to walk without severe pain, I left DeKalb Medical Hospital. I didn't move back into my house because the fear of Fernando catching me home alone frightened and lingered in me, so I stayed at Mom's house. We prayed, read the Bible together and attended church services. The time spent with Mom was much needed. I enjoyed being with her and feeling her love. We bonded and became closer than ever.

I went to the courthouse to get a restraining order against Fernando. The judge granted a T.P.O. (Temporary Protective

Order), ordering Fernando out of my house immediately; he was to stay at least a thousand feet from me or face arrest. The judge also stated, "The order is temporary and can be updated after a year if need be." That same day I had my lawyer to file for divorce, then I stopped by a pawn shop to buy a handgun.

My brothers took turns hanging around Mom's house just in case Fernando decided to show his face. Every few days, I went by my house to check and make sure everything was alright. One day before I changed all the door locks, Fernando sneaked to the house and took away everything he could put his hands on. He took most of the furniture, which he never spent one dime to help buy. He took all the television sets, the stereo system, the microwave, all my jewelry, cut up all my nice clothes, punched big holes in the wall throughout the entire house and cleaned out our joint bank account. I stood in the center of my house thinking, "What a low life." It's a good thing I managed a secret savings account he didn't know about to save a little money for emergencies. Otherwise, I would have been left with nothing. I didn't notify the police because it was a good sign of Fernando getting out my life. In time, I could buy and replace the things he stole or destroyed.

There were no signs of Fernando anywhere after he took everything out of the house. I felt at ease as time passed. I guessed Fernando went into hiding and stayed away because word got out on the street that my brother, Oliver, was looking for him. Mom constantly asked Oliver not to do anything foolish and let the police do their job of handling the situation with Fernando. Oliver promised Mom, "I won't do anything to the coward." Out of all Mom's sons, Oliver could be considered the "wild child." He basically told Mom what she wanted to hear, knowing his words went in one ear and out the other. Oliver was angry and out to get Fernando. The best thing Fernando did was stay in hiding if he knew what Oliver had in store for him.

A month later while sitting in my room contemplating whether to move back into my house, I decided to move back. It was a long mental battle before coming to that conclusion. The holes in the walls were repaired, and I refurnished the house with just enough furniture to make the house presentable until replacing more expensive things.

The first two nights, I found it hard trying to sleep in my own house. My mind played tricks on me, causing me to see images of Fernando standing in the shadows of the dark. The fearful effect Fernando had on me was the reason why I kept the house dimly lit during the night and slept with the handgun in bed under the pillow. I slept light, and I awoke to every little sound I thought I heard.

Nine days after moving back home, I came in from work at Lavon. I took a long hot bath then prepared for bed around 10:30 p.m. Just as I took off my robe and got ready to climb into bed with only panties and a bra on, I heard a noise towards the front part of the house. I leaped to my feet, slipped my hand under the pillow to grab the pistol and slowly crept through the dim hallway investigating. Clearing the hallway and almost paralyzed in fear, I saw Fernando coming from around the kitchen counter towards me. He didn't see the handgun lowered at my side. He stopped for two seconds squinting his eyes to focus on me, then slowly walked towards me and said, "Now, Debra. Did you think you'd get away that easily?" I didn't say anything as Fernando approached me. When he got within three feet in front of me, I raised the handgun pointing it straight at his head.

Frozen in fear, he shouted, "Woe!!! Don't shoot!" With both hands halfway in the air, Fernando didn't move as he watched my hand trembling with the gun held tight and tears rolling down my face.

By my demeanor, he realized he stood face to face with death. He began begging, "Please, please, please don't shoot me." I wasn't a killer, but the fear, anger, frustration, hurt and every negative emotion seemed to swell inside my hand. It was all ready to explode in my trigger finger so I could release built up pressure from my body. I prepared to pull the trigger and catch a murder case if Fernando made the slightest sudden move. A baby grew inside me, and I took responsibility to protect it at any cost. I said without shouting, "If you move another inch, I'll kill you…"

Fernando cowered down at the face of death, becoming a sad and despicable sight to see as a man. His true cowardliness spewed from his pores as he begged and pleaded, "Please, don't kill me, please. I'm sorry for everything I ever did to hurt you. Please, I didn't mean it. I just came here to get something I left…"

I shouted, "Stop lying, sucker, before I put a bullet in you. You already took everything! You came here to kill me. I have a baby inside me and I'll be damned if I let you hurt us!"

Trembling and shaking like a leaf on a tree, Fernando said in a choked voice, "No. I only came..."

Interrupting, I shouted louder, "Shut up, liar, before I make all your family dress in black. Get out of my house right now or else I'll kill you right here!" He backed away slowly and took off running out the side kitchen door like a scary chicken.

I rushed to lock the kitchen door then picked up the telephone to call the police, informing them that Fernando violated the restraining order. A lady at the police station dispatch asked, "Do you want us to send a policeman out to you?"

I declined, "That's okay; he's gone." It was good enough knowing they would be looking to pick him up for violating the restraining order.

She replied, "Well, we'll still need you to come down some-time between now and tomorrow morning to file a complaint." For the first time in a long time, I felt relief from under the stress and pressure of fear. I had prayed and prayed, cried and cried until my tears almost dried up. I made up my mind to fight back and not take the abuse anymore. I said to myself, "If something didn't change, he will end up killing me anyway." I also got a lit-tle confidence from Fred because several days prior, I went to visit him in prison and told him how Fernando physically abused me and that I filed for divorce and bought a handgun. Fred became angry and said, "That chump knows if I was home, he wouldn't try that foolish stunt. If that's the coward he wants to be and put his hands on you again, go ahead and smoke his butt." It surprised me a bit to hear Fred talk like that because over the few years in prison, he became a Christian. I realized his advice went against his belief, and he spoke out of love and concern for me.

He wanted so bad to be there and protect me.

I walked through the house checking all the doors and windows to make sure they were locked. After I finished the call to the police, I walked back to the living room and planned to call Mom and let her know what happened, but I remembered I hadn't checked the sliding glass door behind the living room curtains. I cracked the curtains to the side to check the lock. The sliding door was unlocked and open about three inches. I placed the handgun on a shelf in the wall unit because both hands were needed to close and lock the heavy sliding door. As I slid the door closed and got ready to turn the lock, Fernando startled me by jerking the sliding door back. He pulled on the other side while I tried holding on long enough to lock the door, but couldn't because he was too strong. He pulled the door back in fury and rushed inside the house shouting, "You stinking whore! You're not going to have my baby!" I backed away from the door and ran around the couch away from him. He yelled insults as he came at me, "You dirty slut! Do you think I'm gonna let you get away with putting a gun in my face?!"

My heart pounded rapidly in my chest. Fernando saw I didn't have the gun in my hand, but he didn't see it lying in the wall unit shelf behind him. We played cat and mouse around the couch, and then he chased me around the coffee table. He threw objects at me, but I dodged every one of them. His eyes were bloodshot red, and the more he chased and couldn't catch me, the angrier he became. He paused for a moment to catch his breath. The adrenaline from fear kept me quick, alert and from feeling tired.

I looked at Fernando's face. His eyes were fire red, and he was breathing so hard, smoke appeared to seep from his nostrils. He stood for a moment to catch his breath. Before resuming the chase, he said in a huffing voice, "Heifer, eventually I'm going to catch you, and when I do…" Fernando took off running behind me before finishing his words, and I ran back to the living room circling the couch again. Less than a minute, Fernando grew extremely tired again. I stood at one corner of the couch while Fernando stood at the other end. I could see the handgun on the wall unit shelf over his shoulder. I thought, "When he chases me to the other end of the couch, I'll make my attempt for the gun." As Murphy's Law would have it, Fernando staggered to the side, bumping the wall unit with his shoulder, then took both hands and pushed the wall unit forcefully to the floor sending everything on the shelves flying through the air and onto the floor.

He backed away from the couch staggering like a drunken man. He became dizzier and dizzier as he grabbed his head, squeezing it with both hands to subdue the pain he felt. His blood pressure had risen extremely high, but I wasn't taking any chances because I knew he could have been faking. He tricked me once before so I observed him closely and recognized a heavy thick flow of blood slowly streaming from his nose. Fernando staggered backwards from the couch, wiped the blood from under his nose with his backhand and began begging me for help, "Debra, please help me. Please, something is wrong. I think I'm about to die. Please help me, Debra."

Heavily breathing, he fell to one knee holding on to the couch, trying to pull himself back up from the floor. I still didn't trust him, so I picked up from the floor a ten inch tall mahogany wood statue of a naked African woman, hand-carved in a way depicting and epitomizing the essence of a black woman's beauty and strength. The statue was painted in black lacquer, and covered in a thick coat of shiny acrylic. The top of the statue was carved with the arms high in the air and hands joined together in an angelic arch forming a loop over and around the head. The statue's waistline was small, giving the body deep definition and the naked buttocks and medium size breasts were round and protruding.

I walked slowly towards Fernando with the six pound statue high above my head in the strike position. With each small slow step I took towards him, past events of abuse flashed before my eyes like a movie. By the time I reached arm's distance to Fernando, the anger and frustration built up inside me was so intense that I almost blanked out. All of a sudden I snapped, lost control and went ballistic on Fernando. I repeatedly hit him in the head and face as I beat him to a pulp with the wooden statue. Every time I hit him with the statue, I mentioned a scene of my past abuse. I beat him in rhythm. When the wooden statue hit his head or face, it made a "clunk" sound. Then I'd say, "This is for the time you beat me with the leather belt!" CLUNK! "This is for the times you raped and sexually abused me!" CLUNK! "This is for the times you punched me in the head and face!" CLUNK! "This is for the times you verbally and mentally abused me!" CLUNK! "This is for the times you tried to kill me!" CLUNK! Tears and sweat soaked the circle of my neck as I kept the rhythm going until I got tired and couldn't go any longer. I stood up from over Fernando and called the police to tell them Fernando broke in my house and he might be dead. The police and ambulance rushed out to my house. The sirens woke and alerted the nosy neighbors who stood on the street and side-walk in front of my house looking to see what they could.

The police and ambulance arrived so quickly that I didn't realize I was still in my panties and bra until the police knocked on the door. I ran to put on a robe then returned to let in the police. The police found Fernando lying in a pool of his own blood. They checked his pulse to see if he was dead, but he was still alive, so they put him in the ambulance preparing to rush him to the hospital. Because Fernando's blood pressure was so high, he suffered a stroke and slipped into a coma while I was beating him.

A policeman stayed at my house and questioned me while the ambulance carried Fernando to the hospital. I was completely honest with the officer, explaining everything which led to me brutally beating Fernando the way I did. I thought, "My own mouth is surely going to send me to jail." After the officer wrote a few notes on his pad he asked, "Are you okay? Is there anything I can do for you before I leave?"

Not knowing if he was taking me to jail I answered, "Yeah, I'm alright. Are you going to take me to jail now?"

With compassion, the officer replied, "Oh no. I'm not taking you to jail, Mrs. Jenkins. This is a clear case of self-defense, and he violated a restraining order. You have a right to defend your-self. He came to hurt or possibly kill you, and the cards turned on him. He got what he deserved." He paused for a moment, then wrote a police detective's name on the back of a business card, handed the card to me and said, "The only thing I need you to do is go down to the station tomorrow morning, ask for the person whose name is on the back of my card and give him a complete report. Other than that, you are free to go."

Relieved I wasn't going to jail, I said, "Thank you very much, officer."

I thought I'd feel better after venting all my frustration on Fernando, but I didn't. I looked in the mirror and felt ashamed of myself. I looked down at the blood on my hands and thought, "Look what I've been reduced to. I never dreamed I could be capable of such violence and ill conduct." I looked back into the mirror and said to myself, "I have become just like Fernando." The guilt settled so heavily on me, and I wished to reverse the whole scene of beating Fernando in such a manner. I had to get myself under control and realize what happened is over, and that there was nothing I could do to change it. At that time, the dream about the slaughtered lamb flashed fresh in my mind.

The time came for me to move on with my life. I fell to my knees on the bathroom floor and cried while praying to God for help in putting my life back together. That night in the bathroom, I recommitted my life to God and asked that He would lead and guide me. I prayed that Fernando wouldn't die at my hands because the burden of his death would be too much to handle.

Fernando stayed in a coma for five months, and when he came out of the coma, he was partially paralyzed with no use of his left side and very limited movement on his right side because of the stroke he suffered. When he became well enough to attend divorce court, he was in a wheelchair and in bad shape. He didn't look like the same person.

Oliver, Nikki, Tasha and Mom sat in court with me that day. Nikki saw the sorrow on my face when I looked over at Fernando sitting in the wheelchair, squirming to keep himself sitting upright. Nikki leaned over to whisper in my ear, "Debra, don't feel sorry for that creep. He got what he had coming and now he's not going to lift his hands to hit anybody. This is his medicine for the way he treated you. I told you his day would come."

I sat in court at a table with my lawyer. I was swollen in pregnancy while periodically glancing at Fernando's face, which was twisted as a result of his stroke. I had been afraid for so long, but now I refused to be scared anymore. I looked at Fernando without intimidation as he stared back at me briefly. Though we didn't talk, but being close enough to read his eyes, we were able to communicate through facial expressions. His disposition told me he accepted what he had coming, and he knew what he did to me was wrong. He knew now that if pushed to the limit, I would react. And now that the tables were turned, I sensed he had a little fear of me.

After the divorce hearing, I lowered my head in sorrow and pity for Fernando as I watched a bailiff wheel him out of the courtroom with a few family members trailing him, headed to another courtroom to face criminal charges for violating the restraining order against him.

Fernando was in such bad shape that even the judge felt sorry for him. At the end of the hearing the judge said to Fernando, "Mr. Jenkins, I'm not having you thrown in jail for violating the restraining order against your wife because by the way you look today, I don't think you'll be a threat to anyone. It looks like you've been punished well enough. I guess someone forgot to tell you women are fighting back these days."

I saw the disappointment in Oliver's face because the judge didn't put Fernando in jail. The judge finished the court proceedings then dismissed the court. Fernando lowered his head as his family members wheeled him out of the courtroom.

December 4, 1993 at 11:20 a.m., I gave birth to a beautiful daughter. I named her Diamond. The day I held her in my arms, I realized all I went through with Fernando wasn't a total disaster. It's amazing how something so beautiful and precious can evolve out of such an ugly situation, but that's how God works sometimes. She is my pride and joy. She has soft light brown beautiful exotic eyes, yet such beautiful eyes often remind me of the horrible memories of the man who helped make them. Never is there a day I regret having her. My only regret is her not growing up in a home with both parents feeding and nurturing her in the pipes of love she so rightfully deserves. I wished, for Diamond's sake, that things could have been different. I know how she feels about not having her father around because I grew up without mine.

When Diamond got older, she began spending time with Fernando, but it's not the same as having both parents at home in a loving atmosphere. I often sat wishing I could've broken the cycle of a one-parent home, which my siblings and I experienced as kids growing up. Here it is many years later, and the cycle continues. I'm affected by watching Diamond grow up without her father at home. It's like seeing myself growing up all over again through Diamond's life. I am grateful for the time Fernando spends with Diamond because it does make a difference in her life, even though he hardly ever comes to pick her up to spend time with her.

Diamond seems to be stable and not overly affected that both parents are not together. Though I forgave Fernando, he and I have an understanding that I will not hinder his relationship with Diamond and he can come get her whenever he wishes, (even though I hardly ever received child support.) When he does come for her, he has to wait outside the door and not step one foot inside of my house.

When I ask Diamond, "Honey, how do you feel about life," she often answers, "Life's okay." She always seems to be happy, so things appear to be alright with her. One day I asked her, "What do you feel inside about your father and your relationship with him?"

She replied, "Daddy is cool and I love him. I just wish he could walk straight like a normal person and come home to live with us." (Fernando is no longer in a wheelchair, but the injuries he sustained have given him a permanent reminder: a limp.)

Those last few words she spoke seemed to pierce an ice cold dagger through my heart. I sighed, "Oh no!" I hugged Diamond tight in my arms and kissed the top of her head. I remained silent as some of the negative thoughts tried to reenter my heart.

Stuck in the middle of a huge lake, I rapidly treaded water to keep from sinking. My arms and legs grew tired. Holding my breath, I let my body sink towards the bottom, motionless to relax my arms and legs. After sinking so far down and not being able to hold my breath much longer, I swam back to the top. With wide open eyes, I looked up straight through the clear, crystal water into the beautiful blue sky.

Penetrating the water's surface, I gasped for air and treaded water again, spinning around in a circle hoping to see the shortest distance to shore. Safety seemed so far away, and each shoreline appeared equally far at distance. Fear tried to creep into my heart, but I refused him. I encouraged myself not to panic and to stay calm if I wanted to survive.

My arms and legs grew tired again, so I took a deep breath, relaxed my arms and legs then sank downward. Looking down I saw no bottom, and Fear beckoned again to let him into my heart. Once again I denied him.

No longer able to hold my breath, I looked up and began swimming back to the top. I saw through clear water high in the sky a big, dark cloud shaped in a giant image like the silhouette of the man I saw in my first dream. The dark shaped cloud drifted slowly overhead towards me as the surface water began to rage. The image shadow swept slowly across the lake's surface. I slowed my swimming pace to the top as the dark cloud moved forward at a snail's pace. The dark cloud came closer and closer until it drifted directly over me.

Still under the water, my surroundings turned completely dark. The dark cloud consumed the lightness around me. My eyes stayed stretched open, and I saw nothing but blackness. Slowly, my heart began to thump as though it was artificial, but I fought to control its rhythm. Fear growled to me, "Let go and let me in."

Refusing to be afraid as I floated towards the top, I repeated, "No, no, no. Get away from me!"

Keeping my head facing upward, within seconds I saw a crack of light trailing the back end of the dark, smothering cloud. The light slowly chased the darkness away. The more the dark cloud drifted away from overhead, the more light flooded into my surroundings.

Recognizing my surroundings were coming back to normal and the water was clear once again, there was no feeling of the cold water's temperature I felt while under water, covered by darkness.

I burst through the water's surface, and air rushed through my nostrils and recycled through my lungs as I breathed hard, swallowing big gulps of air. The water's surface ceased its raging. Treading the water rapidly, I spun around in the middle of the lake, looking in all four directions. The shorelines seemed even farther away. "What am I going to do," I thought.

I refuse to die and I will not give up! Remembering I knew how to swim, I began taking strokes. Moderately stroking my arms and legs through the water with both eyes closed, my head turned side to side at each stroke. I couldn't see my way or anything ahead of me, but I continued swimming.

I ignored Fear's voice as he whispered, "Give up, give in. How long do you think you can swim like this before drowning? You'll never make it." Still stroking and never responding to Fear, I whispered to myself, "Yes, I will. I will make it."

The tiredness in my arms and legs began to leave, and I started to gain strength. Harder and harder, I stroked, feeling the power in my arms and legs growing stronger and stronger. As I swam, I could feel my body being slightly lifted above the surface. Opening my eyes, I stopped moving my head side to side and looked straight forward while still stroking. Realizing I was hydroplaning on the water's surface, my body gradually lifted higher and higher. Suddenly, like an airplane taking off on a runway at high speed, my body rose from the water. I put my legs together and spread my arms open wide like a flying bird, and soared high above the earth. Looking downward, the earth got smaller.

The sky was set in a rich, clear blue. Flying high in the sky, the spirit of joy and comfort invaded my entire body, sending tingles and warm, pleasant chills through me. Penetrating up through the thick clouds and smoothly leveling off on my feet, I stood ankle-deep in the middle of a turquoise colored celestial ocean. There were beautiful, greenish-blue waters as far as the eyes could see, and the distance could be touched by just an arm's reach. A playful baby-like joy filled me as I splashed water continually over my head. After hours of unending play, I turned to look behind me and saw the ocean's shore, made of glistening clouds, sparkling in crisp whiteness, radiating golden splendor from its inside.

I lifted up and took to the air again. I began to speak, "Thank you, Lord. Thank you, Jesus. Thank you." The feeling of joy was so intense and overwhelming that I praised the Lord continually while flying high up in the sky. I found myself losing consciousness because of the incomprehensible joy that overtook me. All I could think to do was open my mouth and keep thanking God.

My body began to shake, but I continued to praise God. The shaking became stronger and I stopped talking because of the faint, familiar voice I recognized at a distance over me, "Mommie! Mommie! Wake up! Wake up Mommie!"

I opened my eyes to a daze as my daughter, Diamond, stopped shaking me. I gazed at her for a moment, almost forgetting my dream. "What's the matter, honey," I asked.

Diamond looked down at me and answered with a complex facial expression, "Mommie, you were talking loud in your sleep."

I thought about my dream as the overwhelming pleasure of joy lingered in my heart. I pulled Diamond close to me and hugged her and said, "Mommie is alright. Mommie is going to be alright."

I felt so good. My faith, trust in the Lord and desire to survive exterminated the demons of fear and doubt that so badly wanted to possess and control me. I thought, "It is real! I'm truly free, free at last!"

Chapter 12

HEALING, RECOVERY
AND ADVICE

A lthough my marriage was abusive, I know that God allowed me to survive so that I might be a witness to others. The Bible teaches that we are overcome by the blood of the lamb (Jesus Christ) and by the words of our testimony. So I know I have a lot to share that may be a blessing, or even a life-saver for other ladies who have suffered or continue to suffer abuse.

One valuable lesson I learned from my experience with Fernando came from none other than our beloved relationship guru, Mrs. Mary. It took place three months into my healing and recovery. I drove to Glama-Rama feeling alive, refreshed and so free. I pulled into Glama-Rama's parking lot as the sun beamed and reflected off of the chrome and glass of the cars, shooting almost blinding rays of sunlight. Getting out of the car to go into the salon, I almost missed Mrs. Mary's car. It was only five feet away from me, but the scattered and shooting rays were a bit challenging. Being that it was hot out, it was odd that Mrs. Mary was sitting outside in the car with a scarf wrapped around her head. Stopping in my tracks, I wondered why she sat still, looking straight forward with no movement. Automatically, I assessed two facts: one, Mrs. Mary was deeply troubled, and two, she was hiding something.

She didn't see me standing behind her car. In suspense, I walked to her car window and asked, "Mrs. Mary, are you alright?"

Coming out of her daze, she appeared startled before answering, "Oh…um…yeah, I'm alright."

I could almost see through Mrs. Mary's dark sunglasses because of the bright sun. Still trying to conceal her face, she turned her head forward. "Why are you sitting in the car, and why don't you come in and get your hair done," I asked. It wasn't until the last word dropped from my lips that I realized I shouldn't have asked that question. I was smart enough to know exactly what happened, even though I didn't know the details. Mrs. Mary was too embarrassed to go inside. She probably thought of the gossip that would await her the moment she stepped in the salon and was asked to take off her sunglasses.

Mrs. Mary turned facing me to answer my question. Taking off her sunglasses and revealing her swollen face and two nasty black eyes she replied, "No, Debra. I don't think I'll be going in there today."

"I understand," was all I could think to say as I saw myself in Mrs. Mary's battered face. All my battered past seemed to flash in my mind in a matter of seconds as I watched the tears roll down Mrs. Mary's cheeks. Her tears told the story of my past life of abuse. Oh, how my heart broke and cried for her, and I refused to resist the tears, which began flowing.

We stared silently at each other for several seconds before Mrs. Mary spoke, "My husband beat me up…Debra, I was so wrong on my views about a man being able to beat up a woman." Tears continued flowing from her eyes as she spoke her last words, "Now I know how it feels."

Mrs. Mary gently looked forward, turned the key to her ignition, starting her car. She slowly drove off, leaving me standing alone under the hot sun. I looked up to the sky, wiping my tear stained eyes as I prayed for Mrs. Mary.

Walking into Glama-Rama, I thought about Ann and how I wished she had witnessed the change in Mrs. Mary because it was obvious Mrs. Mary learned a valuable lesson through her own husband's abuse. No doubt, their incident changed her life forever.

Another thought I'd like to share with you comes from a television program I saw. It was about women in the country of India and Pakistan being splashed with gasoline then set ablaze by their sick-minded husbands who didn't want them anymore. I cried uncontrollably because I felt the sad, traumatic pain of the women's abuse while they gave their stories in the television interview. I had been burned and scarred just like them, but in a different way—-not by actual fire, but I was terribly burned by being systematically tortured physically and mentally for a long period of time. Every time I look into a mirror, I see the invisible brand and scars on my forehead from Fernando's abuse.

I never thought a simple memory could bring back so much pain and feel so deeply real. It was inhuman, immoral and evil what I went through in my marriage, all because my husband lacked the understanding of simple human kindness. There are times when chills run up my spine from hearing a movie title like, "Sleeping with the Enemy," or the name of a song title like, "There's a Stranger in my House."

I kept the pain and secret of past abuse hidden in my heart for many years, and it affected and interfered with my subsequent relationships even though the other person didn't have a clue what went on inside me. If only I could've peeped down into the future and into my tomorrow, things in my life would be different; but I couldn't.

It's a battle trying to escape memories of the many times I wore black eyes and sunglasses to hide them, the wearing of makeup to hide scars, bruises and scratches, not to mention medical expenses from seeing physicians because of psychological and physical abuse. The loss of income from not being able to work until I healed from scars and bruises was a burden. Plus, I was reminded of having to replace broken things, and the memory of burned and cut up clothes because of Fernando's rage and jealousy was still very real.

It took God's help to do something I never thought I could do, and that was to forgive Fernando for abusing me. Forgiveness was the condition for healing, recovery and moving on to have a full and peace-filled life. I had to forgive to release all the negative emotions from my heart, which would've caused blockage to my spiritual growth, and great detriment to my health, state of mind, and most importantly, my walk with God.

God allowed certain doors in my life to close. But He opened many, many more doors and blessed me abundantly. Looking back, I realize I could've been dead and gone, but through the grace and mercy of God, He spared my life and changed me for the better during the process. Though Fernando brought me down to the dumps, God reached down, pulled me up and delivered me from the bottomless pits and restored my life, then allowed me to prosper ten times over compared to when I was with Fernando.

During our marriage, I gave Fernando my best and all my love. He tried to convince me I was stupid and crazy, but deep down inside, I knew better. His need to control every part of my life outweighed the respect and concern for me and my needs. But now that's the past. Life goes on, and I moved forward; I don't look back. I must admit there were many times while being abused I wished Fernando got a taste of his own medicine, hoping it would make me feel better. But when he did taste his medicine, it didn't make me feel better because I'm not the kind of person who rejoices at the hurt of others. I am a loving person, and I don't want to think or act towards anyone the way Fernando mistreated me.

There are difficult days, yet there are days when just the mere thought of life's presence looming inside me brings joy and peace to my heart that can't be explained, and I owe all the praises and glory to God Almighty and Jesus Christ, my Lord and Savior.

During the days of abuse, I underwent a strong internal spiritual battle. My flesh pulled hard to one side and tried to defeat and dominate me in fear and depression. Some days, I felt like I wanted to give in, but the spirit in me wouldn't let me. I was a fighter who decided to trust God. As I surrendered to the Lord, my spiritual being gained momentum and strength, pulling me hard to the Lord's side. My faith grew, and I gained a renewed interest and self-confidence, self-esteem and self-worth.

I started attending church regularly and calling on the name of Jesus for healing, rebuilding my life and deliverance from the mental anguish I placed on myself. After doing that, the joy of life returned inside me and I once again felt the free-flowing fountain of life and joy running through my veins. The rivers of self-worth ran like an open dam inside me, and helped rebuild and nourish the character of my true self and who I had hoped to be. I redirected all my emotions towards loving God, loving my daughter, Diamond, and my family. I had thought all the tears shed in the past were in vain, useless and hopeless, but that was never the case because God heard my cry all along. He moved in His own time. At one point, my heart had grown so hard and empty until I realized it would take a miracle to soften it again. That's exactly what happened—-God worked a miracle in my life and He will do the same for you if you trust in Him.

I never thought I'd be so happy to regain my maiden name when my divorce with Fernando became final. My face softened from the release of fear and burdens. I looked and felt like ten years were erased from my age. I feel beautiful and renewed inside once again. I thank God for life because even though I had been badly battered and abused, I am still alive.

I've healed and mentally recovered at least eighty percent. Some women are not as fortunate because they were brutally beaten or murdered some other way by their spouse. I've learned that certain types of abusive attacks are assaults on the soul and spirit of a person, and can only be healed by a spiritual solution.

That's why I firmly advise women to seek help from God first. Pray and keep praying. It may seem as though nothing is happening or changing, but believe me, it is! God is working your situation out for the best.

There are a lot of women experiencing the same things I went through. There was a part deep inside my inner-being Fernando couldn't touch or abuse. Until you refocus, know better and have an attitude to change your circumstances, you will continue living in a sphere of defeat, spiritual emptiness, uneasiness and sorrow. You have to begin lining your life up with the Word of God, finding out what's in your life that hinders your relationship with God and then removing the hindrances. My problem wasn't that I loved Fernando too much. Instead, the problem was that I put Fernando first in my life before God. God must always be first in your life above everything!

Men who beat women are cowards. I often wonder, "How do we get abusive men to see women are beautiful species of God's creation who need to be loved and cared for?" Some women believe if a man doesn't beat her, he doesn't love her. That's absolutely absurd! Anyone who thinks that way really needs to seek help, and that's the hard truth. He doesn't love you if he beats up on you. The first time he beats you, LEAVE! Things will only get worse if you don't. People tried to tell me the same thing while I went through abuse, but I didn't listen well enough to make quick changes. Get away as soon as possible and don't hesitate to call the police. Don't let him isolate you. Most of the time the abusers are extremely afraid to get the authorities involved, even though many of them pretend not to be afraid of the law.

Think about it: a man who loves his car washes, cleans and polishes it really nice to drive around, showing it off as the wheels sparkle and shine in the sunlight. If he starts having car trouble, will he get mad and come home to crash his car into the garage? Think about it for a moment!

There are many abused women who are made housewives, and are convinced they can't survive without their spouse. That's how many women get trapped. Some of them are not able to take care of themselves, nor do they have any income to take care of themselves. Many of them don't have the income to take care of their children, so they have to solely depend on the abuser's income, thus, allowing themselves to endure many days of torture and abuse.

I think more families or parents need to be more patient and sensitive with abused spouses because they really don't know what they are going through mentally, physically and emotionally. The spouse is in constant fear for life, knowing if her mate badly abuses her, he's capable of killing her at any time.

My advice is to get family members and friends involved when abused. Go to a women's shelter if need be, or go live with a relative. Today in the news, women are being killed by their spouses more now than ever, and this is a violent epidemic plaguing American cities. It must stop!

Before my divorce, I maintained good credit and implemented a "Plan B," and I still do in my whole way of life because during my days with Fernando, life taught me to save for hard times. I've learned never go too deep into situations where I can't get out if need be.

Over the years, I witnessed battered women turn to alcohol abuse, drug abuse, suicide and suffer nervous breakdowns. I have seen where some women who had a child through an abusive marriage or relationship found it hard to love the child. Some women ended up hating the child and preferred to give the child up for adoption. Remember, "It's not the child's fault!"

Fernando hurt me in many ways, and in some ways I don't have words to describe the horrific behavior and deceit of the man who claimed to love me, who managed to fool others around him into believing he was a sane, rational being. Yet, I refused to let that stop me from loving my child. Life taught me when you don't see any way out, God is there and when everything is removed out of my life, God is still there.

All in all, I've learned so much about living and it's only my faith and trust in the Lord that enables me to keep on moving ahead in life. I remember the day the Lord delivered me. I was set free, free to walk out of the prison of fear and abuse, which held me for so long. I am free to breathe, live again and know the joy of life again. Some days, I feel so good inside that I can almost hear my spirit shout, "Roll out the red carpet and sound the alarms because I'm free!" Yet, some days, I struggle a little with my past, but I never stop praying and trusting God.

My final words to my sisters: when men say they love you, just remember I told you, "Video is better than audio. They can prove their love by actions because love will never permit itself to abuse anyone." Also remember this, no matter what comes at you, even though it may defeat you, it will not define you. God bless you!

Wood statue of a naked African woman referred to on page 210.

Recognizing the Signs of an
Abusive Relationship

1. Has your spouse forced you to have sex or caused you pain sexually without your consent?
2. Does your partner criticize you constantly, verbally degrade you or blame you for things that may have not been your fault?
3. Has your spouse ever slapped, bitten, kicked, pushed, or thrown objects at you because he or she was upset?
4. Does your spouse sometimes act jealous or suspicious of you?
5. Does your spouse occasionally accuse you of having affairs?
6. Does your spouse make it hard for you to see family and friends, and does he or she monitor your mail, phone calls, and personal space?
7. Does your spouse threaten to hurt you, your family, friends, children, pets or property from time to time?
8. Does your partner have a history of violence in previous relationships?

If you have answered yes one or more times, then you are in an abusive relationship. Here is information that may help:

National Coalition Against Domestic Violence
www.ncadv.org
1-800-799-SAFE (-7233 for a translator)

ABOUT THE AUTHOR
Women's Advocate, Author, Entrepreneur

After spending two years in an abusive marriage, Debra Williamson has victoriously evolved into one of the nation's most provocative advocates for women's rights. To that end, she has committed her life to encouraging other women who are victims. A milestone in her journey is the publishing of her story, *Concealed Deception: A Courageous Woman's Journey From Abuse to Triumph*. Co-authored with her brother, Fred, *Concealed Deception* promises to be a source of encouragement to victims of domestic violence and those who love them.

Debra is an active member of New Birth Missionary Church in Lithonia, Georgia, where she now lives. A native of Fort Lauderdale, Florida, she is the proud mother of one beautiful daughter, Diamond. Debra spent most of her childhood in Nassau, Bahamas, which was her parents' native land and their choice for raising their children. The fourth of six children in a closely-knit family, she has great reverence for the importance of family values.

Debra has maintained a cosmetology license for the past 25 years, as well as a real estate broker license. She has owned her own hair salons, and today she serves as the owner of Caldwell Brokers Real Estate, wherein she utilizes 11 years of expertise in making families' dream of home ownership a reality. She takes pride in the fact that her business has afforded her the opportunity to mold aspiring agents who want to be brokers. She has imparted her wisdom to many people in this profession.

Booking Information

To arrange a speaking engagement or an appearance, contact the author at:

www.debrawilliamson.com

or email her at

williamsonde@comcast.net

to get more information, call

678-984-8563